Other Books Authored by Barbara Frone:

<u>My Journey With God</u>
published by Westbow Press 5/2010

RESTING IN JESUS

*How to Live a Powerful, Amazing,
and Victorious Life*

"There remaineth therefore a rest to the people of God. For he that is entered into his rest, he also hath ceased from his own works, as God did from his." Hebrews 4:9-10

BARBARA FRONE

WESTBOW®
PRESS
A DIVISION OF THOMAS NELSON
& ZONDERVAN

All Bible verses are from the King James Bible.

WestBow Press books may be ordered through booksellers or by contacting:

WestBow Press
A Division of Thomas Nelson & Zondervan
1663 Liberty Drive
Bloomington, IN 47403
www.westbowpress.com
1 (866) 928-1240

ISBN: 978-1-4908-4135-9 (sc)
ISBN: 978-1-4908-4137-3 (hc)
ISBN: 978-1-4908-4136-6 (e)

Library of Congress Control Number: 2014911047

Printed in the United States of America.

WestBow Press rev. date: 06/23/2014

CONTENTS

This book is dedicated to God, the lover of my soul.

"For God so loved the world, that he gave his only begotten Son, that whosoever believeth in him should not perish, but have everlasting life." John 3:16

Follow Barbara on one of her Facebook pages:
BARBARA WALKER FRONE
A DAY IN MY LIFE WITH GOD
LET YOUR WORD BE LIFE MINISTRIES

AUTHOR'S TESTIMONY

"But thanks be to God, which giveth us the victory through our Lord Jesus Christ." 1 Corinthians 15:57

I started attending church on a regular basis in September of 1989. I was 26 years old then. In December of 1989, I accepted Jesus Christ as my Savior and was baptized in March of 1990. I was living the Christian life or at least how I thought a Christian life should be lived. I attended church three times a week, took notes on all the sermons, taught Sunday school, worked in the bus ministry, listened to Christian music some, read my Bible some, and prayed some.

Nine years later, I quit going to church. When people asked me why I quit going to church, I would always answer them, "I needed a break." I didn't realize until now how true that was. I did indeed need a break. I needed a break from trying to change myself. I needed a break from trying to make myself do right. I wore myself out trying to live how I thought a Christian should live. Most of the time I felt like a failure because I was not doing all I thought a Christian should be doing.

God did let me have a break until March of 2008. My whole story is in my book, <u>MY JOURNEY WITH GOD</u>, but here it is in a nutshell. In March of 2008, God used my daughter to say some things to me which led me to doubt my salvation. I wanted to be sure I was still saved, so I started praying and reading my Bible again. To my amazement, every verse I read told me that I was not only saved, but I was saved forever! I started attending church again. But this time, I told myself I would not do anything including changing myself unless God put it on my heart.

From then until now, God has taught me many truths that have set me free from trying to live the Christian life. He has taught me to take my eyes off of myself and keep them on Jesus. He has taught me to rest in Jesus and stop trying to make myself into a perfect Christian. He has taught me while I am beholding Jesus' beauty and grace, I am changing into his image effortlessly. He has taught me he wants to live his life through me and if I let him, I would live a powerful, amazing, and victorious life.

My prayer for all who read this book is that you will also be set free from trying to live the Christian life and let Jesus live a powerful, amazing, and victorious life through you.

Chapter 1

HIS OBEDIENCE, NOT YOURS

"For as by one man's disobedience many were made sinners, so by the obedience of one shall many be made righteous." Romans 5:19

As she drove away from the church, she knew she was not coming back. After nine years of attending church there, she was worn out. Even her husband asked her almost every Sunday after she came home from church, "Why do you keep going there? You always come home all mentally beat up." "I go because it is the right thing to do," she thought to herself. "I go because I want to please God."

But that Sunday she did not want to do it anymore. She was tired. She was worn out. She needed a break. In fact, that is exactly what she told everybody who asked her why she stopped going to church, "I needed a break." She even took a break from reading the Bible, because every time she read it, she heard the preaching in her mind that she had been listening to for the past nine years. "You need to do this. You need to do that. You need to throw that away. You need to dress this way. You need to live this way. You need to be pure and holy." Oh, sometimes she succeeded in following these rules, but more often than not, she had failed.

In fact, she felt like a failure most of the time. She did not know it then, but she was living a defeated Christian life, because her eyes were always on her obedience or the lack thereof, instead of on Christ's obedience. So every time she felt like she had obeyed, she was elated, but every time she felt like she had failed, she was depressed.

In 2 Corinthians 10:5, it says, *"Casting down imaginations, and every high thing that exalteth itself against the knowledge of God, and bringing into captivity every thought to the obedience of Christ."* If she would have kept her mind on Christ's obedience, her obedience would have flowed out of her effortlessly. In Matthew 6, it says, *"But seek ye first the kingdom of God and his righteousness; and all these things shall be added unto you."* She should have kept her mind off of her righteousness, and put all of her focus on Jesus' righteousness.

Jesus' righteousness was her foundation. It was the rock she should have stood on. It was the place she should have always come back to, especially after she had failed. If she had kept her mind on Jesus' righteousness, instead of her righteousness, all the things she sought after, including living right, would have been added to her effortlessly.

This story is my story, but it could just as well be the story for many Christians. God has since set me free. I no longer live a defeated Christian life, and you will not either, if you keep your eyes on Christ's obedience instead of on your obedience. It is not about you. It is about Jesus! His obedience made you righteous. His obedience will keep you righteous. In fact, all spiritual warfare is based on the devil making you focus on yourself, your thoughts, and your deeds. It is painful to be self-occupied. God wants you to be Christ occupied. Preachers feel if they do not preach against sin, people will continue to sin, but preaching against sin keeps people's minds on sin. Preachers need to preach about God's grace. I have found the more I know about God's grace, the less attracted I am to sin and the more attracted I am to Jesus. It is the goodness of God that leads to repentance.

If I had to tell you in one sentence of how to live a powerful, amazing and victorious life, I would tell you to let go of all your striving and to rest in Christ. To rest in Christ is a simple statement, but for most of us, it is not so easy to do because we think if we are not striving, nothing will be accomplished. We think we need to be striving to become a better Christian or striving to please God, but Galatians 3:3, says *"Are ye so foolish? having begun in the Spirit, are ye now made perfect by the flesh?"* What this means is you should not strive to change yourself into what you think is the perfect Christian.

Part of resting in Christ means to let Jesus make the changes in you that need to be made. This is very, very important for you to understand, because if you start making changes in yourself, you still think you can please God by your works. There is a great example of this in Genesis when the first two sons of Adam and Eve brought their offering to God. Cain brought harvest from his garden, the fruit of his hands and this displeased God, because Cain thought he could please God by bringing his works. But his brother, Abel brought a lamb and this pleased God because it was a picture of Christ who, the Bible says, was slain before the foundation of the world.

It is all about the sacrifice you bring. It is not about you. It is all about Jesus, our perfect sacrifice. In the Old Testament, when the Israelites brought their sacrifice to the priest, the priest did not examine them, he examined their sacrifice to make sure it had no spots or blemishes. In the New Testament, we come before God in the name of Jesus, and just as the priest did in the Old Testament, God examines our sacrifice, not us. It is not about us. It is not about what we did, or did not do. It is all about what Jesus did on the cross.

Another reason why you should not work on changing yourself is because if you succeed in changing a particular area in your life, you will have a tendency to feel like you are better than those who have not succeeded in that area. And if you fail, you will not only feel like a failure, but you will also feel guilty for failing. In fact, you will probably think God is angry with you, which will cause you to withdraw from him. If you live your life by trying to change yourself into what you think a perfect Christian should be, you will live a defeated Christian life. One day you will be up. The next day you will be down. So if you want to live a powerful, amazing and victorious life, rest in Christ by letting him make changes in you. If you let Jesus make changes in you, he will not only succeed, but afterwards you will feel grateful and humbled because you know it was not you. It was all him!

So now that you understand you are not to change anything about yourself, you must be thinking, "Then what exactly do I do?" You start walking with God every day, just like Adam did in the garden of Eden. Talk to him. Ask him questions. Bare your soul to him. While you are walking with God, you will get to know him. Read his Word. His Word is all about Jesus. Get to know Jesus, because in 1 John 4:17, it says, *"As he is, so are we in this world."* Everything the Bible says about Jesus, pertains to you, because as he is, so are you in this world, not when you get to heaven.

Another part of walking with God is letting his Spirit lead you. First John 4:15, says, *"Whosoever shall confess that Jesus is the Son of God, God dwelleth in him, and he in God."* When you accepted Jesus Christ as your Savior, God's Spirit moved inside of your spirit. God gave you his Spirit to walk you through this life. This is why the Bible says God will never leave you nor forsake you, because his Spirit is always with you. You are never alone. God gave you his Spirit to lead you and to teach you truth.

John 16:13, says, *"Howbeit when he, the Spirit of truth, is come, he will guide you into all truth: for he shall not speak of himself; but whatsoever he shall hear, that shall he speak: and he will shew you things to come."* As you spend time with God and in his Word, you will learn to hear his voice. God's voice is always gentle. You will never feel rushed or forced. He will never manipulate you or condemn you. Throughout your day listen for God's voice. He wants to talk to you. He wants you to get to know him. He wants to give you direction. He wants to give you wisdom. He wants to answer your questions.

You walk with God by reading his Word every day. Every word in the Bible contains truth. Every time you read it, the Holy Spirit will reveal truth he wants you to know at this moment in time. Do not worry about where to start reading or what you do not understand. Keep reading and concentrate on what you do understand. Isaiah 55:11, says, *"So shall my word be that goeth forth out of my mouth: it shall not return unto me void, but it shall accomplish that which I please, and it shall prosper in the thing whereto I sent it."* Even though you may not understand what you are reading, the words you are reading are still going to accomplish whatever God wants them to accomplish in you.

John 1:1, says the Word is Jesus, so never look at the Bible as a rule book or a guide of how you should live. Always look for Jesus. Expect him to give you revelation. Expect him to reveal things he has for you to see. It is like being in a church service and even though everyone hears the same sermon, everyone will receive a different message in their spirit depending on what God is teaching them at the moment. This is so important for you to understand, because if you start looking at the Bible as a set of rules to follow, you will again try to change yourself. The temptation to change yourself will be very strong at first, but it will get easier with time. You will learn to rest in Jesus. You will learn to let Jesus live through you.

You are on a beautiful journey with your Savior. This journey is a lifetime journey, so do not be in a hurry. You will often be tempted to make changes on your own. Do not do it. We have a tendency to want radical change, but change takes time. God is not in a hurry, so slow down and enjoy this journey. If you are struggling, talk to Jesus. Always get direction from him. In fact, this will help you. Do not look at yourself at all. Always look at Jesus. The devil will constantly try to get you to look at yourself. If you do something wrong, he will try to get you to condemn yourself. If you do something right, he will get you to think you did not do enough. Or the devil will get you to think about how good you are or how bad you are, or even how good or bad others are. Anything to keep your mind off of Jesus. But the Bible says in Romans 3:12 that none of us are good, so stop trying to be good or thinking about how good you or others are. If you could please God by being good, you would not need Jesus. And since you are saved, you cannot be bad, because you are the righteousness of God in Christ.

The battle is not only in your mind, it is for your mind. Jesus wants your mind to stay on him, because that is where your victory is. Isaiah

26:3, says, *"Thou wilt keep him in perfect peace, whose mind is stayed on thee: because he trusteth in thee."* The devil wants your mind to stay on you, because if your mind is stayed on you, he can keep you running between feeling full of pride one day to feeling like a failure the next.

What your mind is thinking about is so important, because whatever you are thinking about will affect your mental and physical health. The Bible says, as a man thinketh, so is he. You become what you think you are. That is why it is so important for you to think about Jesus and all that he is, because as he is, so are you in this world. Jesus is righteous and so are you! Jesus is blessed and so are you! Jesus is seated on the right hand of the Father and so are you! It does not matter what you see or how you feel. What you see and how you feel are part of your natural world. God wants you to live above your natural world in the supernatural where he is.

Your mind is a tremendous tool. It can take you to the beach even though you are sitting at a desk. It can take you back in time to when you were a little child. It can take you into the future as you dream about where you are going to retire. And it can take you from the natural into the supernatural. This is where faith comes in. You do not need faith to follow a set of rules. But you do need faith to believe you are the righteousness of God in Christ, even though you do not feel righteous. You do need faith to believe you still have right standing with God, even though you just messed up big time. You do need faith to believe you can still come boldly before God, even though you just cursed at someone or you just had a horrible thought.

In 2 Kings 6:8–23, there is a story about an Old Testament prophet named Elisha. The king of Syria was setting up camps in order to trap the Israelites, but Elisha would always warn the king of Israel, who would then go around the camps to avoid the traps. This troubled the king of Syria because he thought his own officers were tipping off the king of Israel, but when he asked his officers who it was tipping off the Israelites, one of them told him about Elisha. So the king of Syria sent his army to capture Elisha. One morning after Elisha's servant woke up and went outside, he looked up and saw the city was surrounded by the Syrian army. He ran back inside to tell Elisha, and when he asked Elisha, what are we going to do, here is how Elisha answered him, *"Fear not: for they that be with us are more than they that be with them. And Elisha prayed, and said, Lord, I pray thee, open his eyes, that he may see. And the Lord opened the eyes of the young man; and he saw: and, behold, the mountain was full of horses and chariots of fire round about Elisha."* My prayer for you as you spend time with God and in his Word is that God would open up your eyes, so the supernatural world will become more real to you than what you see in the natural.

I recommend you start a journal where you write things down God is teaching you throughout this journey. God has much to tell you. God wants to do great and mighty works through your life. Throughout your journey with him, God will teach you to let go. He will teach you to let go of all your guilty feelings. He will teach you to let go of all your worries. He will teach you to let go of all your fears. He will help you unclutter your mental and physical world by showing you things that are not a part of your destiny. He will teach you to live a life free to be who you are in Christ. It may be hard for you to let go at first, because you are afraid to trust God. You are afraid he is going to do something you do not like. If you stop and think about this, where do you think this type of thinking is coming from? It is coming from the devil. The Bible says in 1 Peter 5:8, *"Be sober, be vigilant; because your adversary the devil, as a roaring lion, walketh about, seeking whom he can devour."* Then in Proverbs 19:12, it says, *"The king's wrath is as a roaring lion; but his favour is as dew upon grass."* These two verses are telling you the devil is trying to devour you by making you believe God is angry with you. But think about it. God was never angry with you. God is angry at sin and he let out all of his anger for sin on the cross when your sin was put on Jesus. When you accepted Jesus Christ as your Savior, you accepted that all your sin was put on Jesus and all his righteousness was put on you. You are now righteous before God always!

In 2 Corinthians 11:3, it says, *"But I fear, lest by any means, as the serpent beguiled Eve through his subtilty, so your minds should be corrupted*

7

from the simplicity that is in Christ." Many people think the Christian life is complicated, but that is a lie from the devil. The devil works through people to complicate things. The Christian life is simple. You rest in what Jesus did for you on the cross, which simply means you know who you are in Christ and you know all the benefits of that position. You walk daily with your Heavenly Father, trusting he is teaching you and guiding you. The rest of the chapters in this book are going to go deeper into what it means to rest in Christ, which will help you live a powerful, amazing and victorious life.

Additional verses to meditate on:

"My soul, wait thou only upon God; for my expectation is from him. He only is my rock and my salvation: he is my defence; I shall not be moved. In God is my salvation and my glory: the rock of my strength, and my refuge, is in God. Trust in him at all times; ye people, pour out your heart before him: God is a refuge for us. Selah." Psalm 62:5-8

"I will greatly rejoice in the Lord, my soul shall be joyful in my God; for he hath clothed me with the garments of salvation, he hath covered me with the robe of righteousness, as a bridegroom decketh himself with ornaments, and as a bride adorneth herself with her jewels." Isaiah 61:10

"And he said unto me, My grace is sufficient for thee: for my strength is made perfect in weakness. Most gladly therefore will I rather glory in my infirmities, that the power of Christ may rest upon me." 2 Corinthians 12:9

"Christ hath redeemed us from the curse of the law, being made a curse for us: for it is written, Cursed is every one that hangeth on a tree: That the blessing of Abraham might come on the Gentiles through Jesus Christ; that we might receive the promise of the Spirit through faith." Galatians 3:13-14

"Blessed be the God and Father of our Lord Jesus Christ, who hath blessed us with all spiritual blessings in heavenly places in Christ." Ephesians 1:3

Chapter 2

GOD LOVES YOU WITH RECKLESS EXTRAVAGANCE

"For I am persuaded, that neither death, nor life, nor angels, nor principalities, nor powers, nor things present, nor things to come, nor height, nor depth, nor any other creature, shall be able to separate us from the love of God, which is in Christ Jesus our Lord." Romans 8:38-39

Springtime was finally here. I was able to put on my new spring coat I purchased a year ago at Burlington Coat Factory in San Francisco. As I was putting it on, it took my mind back to the day I purchased it. When I first tried on this coat, I could not decide between the orange or green one. I went back and forth, and finally decided to buy the green coat. Today, a year later, I wished I had bought both coats. A few weeks after thinking this, I was visiting my mom in Texas. She took me to the Burlington Coat Factory, I think it was in Austin, but I'm not sure. As I was walking past the winter coats, I thought about the orange coat I secretly wished I had bought. I say secretly because I never mentioned it to anybody, nor did I ask God for it. Then as I was walking towards the spring coats, I thought to myself, "Just maybe the same coat in orange will be there." But just as quickly, another thought interrupted me, "The style of just about everything changes every year. It would be a miracle if that same coat was still available and in the same colors one year later." Then all of a sudden I saw them. The same coats in the same colors as last year! The orange coat was there. The exact same one! I was overwhelmed with joy. Our Heavenly Father loves us with reckless extravagance! He loves to surprise us. He loves to give us gifts.

During that same visit with my mom in Texas, I was looking for new dress pants. I tried on so many, but none of them fit right. I was getting discouraged. Then a few days before I was to fly back home to Alaska, we went to Dillard's. Dillard's is a high end store in the malls in the south. As I was looking through their dress pants, I noticed they had my size in several colors and in extra long, which you hardly ever see in stores. Usually, if you need extra long pants, you have to order them. I tried on several pair of pants. They all fit like a glove! Now for the best part. This is Dillard's. Nothing is cheap in Dillard's. I would have easily paid $80 to $100 for each pair of these pants in an upscale store like this. But my Heavenly Father brought me another miracle that day. Each pair of pants, and I bought five of them, were only $35. I did not think I was seeing correctly, but yes, each pair of pants was only $35. Everything important to us is important to our Heavenly Father!

You have to feel this reckless extravagant love God has for you right now where you are to have the power to become what God wants you to become. Children who are loved by their parents feel secure. They are not afraid because they know that no matter what they do, their parents will love them and will always be there for them. When children feel confident in their parent's love for them, they feel accepted and free to be who they are. God wants you to feel the same way about his love for you. He wants you to feel secure in his love. He wants you to be confident in his love for you. In fact, he wants you to feel so confident in his love for you that you will always come boldly to him for whatever you need, because you know he loves you with reckless extravagance. He always wants you to run to him for everything, especially after you have failed.

Many Christians run the other way after they mess up. They feel God is upset with them. Never, never run away from God. You need his love the most after you have messed up. God loves you! He loves you unconditionally! He loves you with reckless extravagance! The Bible says perfect love casts out fear. When you feel secure in God's perfect love, all of your fears will fall away. God loves you so much that when you accepted Jesus Christ as your Savior, his Spirit moved inside of your spirit, so you would never be alone again. His Spirit wants to restore you, lead you, guide you, teach you, and comfort you.

Too many preachers think if they only preach about God's love, people will not stop sinning. Too many preachers think if they do not tell people they need to change, they will never change. Too many preachers are thinking wrong. It is God's reckless extravagant love for us that melts away all guilt and condemnation inside of our souls. It is the revelation of God's love that gives us the power to sin no more. It is the revelation of his love that draws us to him. It is the revelation of his love that makes us not want to sin no more.

I believe many Christians feel God only loves them when they are doing right. They feel God gets upset with them when they mess up, especially when they mess up on purpose. Then they run away from God, because they do not believe he could continue to love them after what they just did. They probably say to themselves, "I am born again. I am not supposed to want to sin. What is wrong with me? How can God love me?" I want you to know you can be set free from this way of thinking.

The only way you will be able to live a powerful, amazing and victorious life is if you live free from all guilt and condemnation. Romans 8:1, says, *"There is therefore no condemnation to them which are in Christ Jesus."* And John 3:17, says, *"For God sent not his Son into the world to condemn the world; but that the world through him might be saved."* Think about it. How can you live a powerful, amazing and victorious life if you feel guilty or condemned most of the time?

I have found that the best way to get rid of guilt and condemnation in your soul is to look for God's reckless extravagant love in your life

11

everyday. Every time you feel guilty or condemned about anything, think about what Jesus did on the cross. Remind yourself it is only a feeling and not the truth. When Jesus died on the cross, he died as you. Jesus and you (your sin nature) were condemned on the cross. It is now finished in God's eyes. Jesus paid it all!!! Jesus cannot be condemned again, and since you are in Christ, neither can you. When Christ died on the cross, so did you. When Christ rose from the dead, so did you. You rose with a divine nature, Christ's. You rose with a new identity in Christ. You rose as a new creature in Christ. When Christ sat down at the right hand of the Father, so did you. You now live your life resting in Christ.

In 2 Corinthians 5:21, it says, *"For he hath made him to be sin for us, who knew no sin; that we might be made the righteousness of God in him."* Jesus' righteousness was imputed unto you the moment you accepted him as your Savior. You are the righteousness of God in Christ, so stop trying to make yourself righteous. The Bible says all of our righteousness is as filthy rags. So no matter how much you try to clean yourself up, your righteousness will still be as filthy rags in God's eyes. In Matthew 6:33 it says that we need to seek his righteousness, not our own.

Once you are rooted and grounded in God's reckless extravagant love for you, you will start to notice a confidence you have never had before. You will start to notice a boldness you have never had before. One thing I have noticed from listening to powerful preachers is they all have a boldness not only in their preaching, but in the way they approach God. They come boldly to the throne of grace in their time of need. They are not ashamed. They walk in confidence knowing God loves them no matter what. They walk in confidence knowing they are righteous in God's eyes. They are bold as a lion because they are secure in who they are in Christ.

Do not just think you are righteous. Know you are righteous! Know you are loved with reckless extravagance! Know you are forgiven! Know you bring your Heavenly Father exceeding joy! Know you can have intimate communion with your Heavenly

Father! If you know who you are in a Christ, you will not be full of pride because you know it is not because of anything you did, but because of everything Jesus did. If you know who you are in Christ, you will not be shy, because you are a child of the Most High God and he said you can come boldly to his throne. If you know who you are in Christ, you will be humble, because you know it is not you, but Christ living through you.

I will close with a conversation I had with God not too long ago. "Father, today while I was walking to the coffee shop, I passed a man that reminded me of my Uncle Heinz from Germany. I thought about how much I loved him as a little child and how much I felt loved by him. Then I thought about what my mother told me about him when I got older. Apparently he was not a very nice man, but I did not know anything about that when I was a little girl. I just knew I loved him and he loved me." Right after I said this, I felt God put on my heart: That is how I love you and that is how I want you to love me. I love you for who you are, my child, just as your uncle loved you for who you were, his niece. You loved your uncle for who he was, your uncle, and I want you to love me for who I am, your Heavenly Father. You trusted your uncle because you were a child, and I want you to trust me because you are my child.

Once your sin has been dealt with by the blood of Jesus, sin can no longer separate you from the reckless extravagant love your Heavenly Father has for you. Do not let anything in this world separate you from his love.

Additional verses to meditate on:

"The blessing of the Lord, it maketh rich, and he addeth no sorrow with it." Proverbs 10:22

"But as it is written, Eye hath not seen, nor ear heard, neither have entered into the heart of man, the things which God hath prepared for them that love him." 1 Corinthians 2:9

"But God, who is rich in mercy, for his great love wherewith he loved us, Even when we were dead in sins, hath quickened us together with Christ, (by grace ye are saved;) And hath raised us up together, and made us sit together in heavenly places in Christ Jesus: That in the ages to come he might shew the exceeding riches of his grace in his kindness toward us through Christ Jesus." Ephesians 2:4-7

"That Christ may dwell in your hearts by faith; that ye, being rooted and grounded in love, May be able to comprehend with all saints what is the breadth, and length, and depth, and height; And to know the love of Christ, which passeth knowledge, that ye might be filled with all the fulness of God." Ephesians 3:17-19

"But my God shall supply all your need according to his riches in glory by Christ Jesus." Philippians 4:19

"We love him, because he first loved us." 1 John 4:19

Chapter 3

START WALKING WITH GOD

"He hath shewed thee, O man, what is good; and what doth the Lord require of thee, but to do justly, and to love mercy, and to walk humbly with thy God." Micah 6:8

In the garden of Eden God walked with Adam every day. God loved walking with Adam. I can only imagine what God and Adam talked about. God knew Adam, so I am sure it was mostly Adam asking God questions. God longs to walk with you, too. He longs to teach you about himself. He longs to show you how much he loves you. The Bible says God created us for his pleasure. God wants a relationship with you.

Of course, you cannot physically walk with God today like Adam did, instead you walk spiritually with him. Walking with God spiritually means talking to him, even though you cannot see him. It means spending time in his Word. Walking with God is like an exercise program. You cannot sit there and watch the instructor and expect to get the benefits. You cannot watch your pastor or your friend walk with God and expect to get the benefits. You have to get up and start walking yourself.

In your walk with God, there is a part for God and a part for you. God's part is to teach you and to lead you. Your part is to walk with him every day. God will meet you wherever you are, but then he wants you to walk with him. He will never leave your side while you are walking with him. He will always gently and patiently lead you down the path he has chosen just for you. You have a calling on your life. You have a purpose in this life. How do you find out what your calling is? How do you know what your purpose is? While you are walking with God, he will put the calling in your heart as desires and passions, and those desires and passions will lead you directly to your purpose.

Five years ago, God put a calling in my heart. I thought it was going to happen right away, but I have since learned before God lets you walk in that calling, you go through what I call "the school of God." During this time God will teach you to let go and completely trust in him. He will teach you to not get offended. He will teach you to depend on him for everything and never look to people to meet your needs. God wants to strengthen your faith muscles. He will test you and try you to make sure you are trusting only in him.

The stronger your walk gets with God, the more opposition you will face. I heard a preacher once say, "With every new level, there is a new devil." That is a true statement. God wants to make sure you are resting in Jesus. He wants to make sure you are grounded in his love, so no matter what opposition you face, you will not lose your confidence in him.

I used to be afraid God would ask me to do something I did not really want to do. I remember once hearing a missionary at my church say something to the effect that he did not care for a certain kind of people and those were the very people God called him to minister to. After I heard that, I was even more afraid of what God would ask of me. I was afraid he would ask me to do something I really disliked and then I would be miserable for the rest of my life. I now know this was a lie from the devil, who the Bible calls the father of lies. According to Psalm 37:4-5, *"Delight thyself also in the LORD; and he shall give thee the desires of thine heart. Commit thy way unto the LORD; trust also in him; and he shall bring it to pass,"* God first puts his desires for your life in your heart and then he gives you those desires. You will never be miserable walking with God!

If you have not started walking with God, start walking with him today. As you talk to him and read his Word, you may become increasingly aware of your shortcomings. You might even feel like you are not good enough for God. This happened to me in my walk with God and this is what he put on my heart: While I am walking with him, the things in my life are just as they should be. He told me not to fret about anything. Those things that are bothering me right now might not be there a year from now. God put on my heart to take my eyes off of myself and keep my eyes on him. In Isaiah 26:3, it says, *"Thou wilt keep him in perfect peace, whose mind is stayed on thee: because he trusteth in thee."* Be conscious of God's Spirit dwelling inside of you. Listen for his leading. Watch for his teachings. Go to him for comfort. If you just sit there and do not start walking with God, nothing much will happen in your life. Things start to happen the moment you start walking with God.

Additional verses to meditate on:

"For as many as are led by the Spirit of God, they are the sons of God." *Romans 8:14*

"Being confident of this very thing, that he which hath begun a good work in you will perform it until the day of Jesus Christ." *Philippians 1:6*

"For by grace are ye saved through faith; and that not of yourselves: it is the gift of God: Not of works, lest any man should boast." *Ephesians 2:8-9*

"For God hath not given us the spirit of fear; but of power, and of love, and of a sound mind." *2 Timothy 1:7*

"But if we walk in the light, as he is in the light, we have fellowship one with another, and the blood of Jesus Christ his Son cleanseth us from all sin." *1 John 1:7*

Chapter 4

YOUR WALK WITH GOD

"The Lord is my shepherd; I shall not want. He maketh me to lie down in green pastures: he leadeth me beside the still waters. He restoreth my soul: he leadeth me in the paths of righteousness for his name's sake. Yea, though I walk through the valley of the shadow of death, I will fear no evil: for thou art with me; thy rod and thy staff they comfort me. Thou preparest a table before me in the presence of mine enemies: thou anointest my head with oil; my cup runneth over. Surely goodness and mercy shall follow me all the days of my life: and I will dwell in the house of the Lord for ever." *Psalm 23:1-6*

The words of Psalm 23 are probably the most widely known words in the Bible. One day as I was meditating on this Psalm, the Holy Spirit put on my heart that this Psalm is a picture of our walk with him. Let's walk through this Psalm together.

The LORD is my shepherd; I shall not want.

The moment you accept Jesus Christ as your Savior, he becomes your Shepherd who will lead you, guide you, take care of you, comfort you, and protect you, so you shall have no lack in any area of your life.

He maketh me to lie down in green pastures.

One of the first things the Lord tells you to do is to lie down in green pastures. In other words, REST. He wants you to enter into his rest. He wants you to rest in him. He never wants you to be restless.

He leadeth me beside the still waters.

The Lord then leads you beside waters of rest. The primary way he leads you is with rest or unrest. He leads you with the presence or absence of peace in your soul.

He restoreth my soul.

Every time you mess up, the Lord restores you. Every time you are cast down, he breathes back life into you.

He leadeth me in the paths of righteousness for his name's sake.

Notice there is more than one path. As a shepherd takes their sheep to different areas during the day for different purposes like grazing or watering, your Shepherd leads you down paths for different purposes. When the Lord leads you, he will always lead you to hope. The paths of righteousness will always lead you to victory. When the Lord leads you, you will always end up doing the right thing at the right time.

Yea, though I walk through the valley of the shadow of death, I will fear no evil: for thou art with me.

Notice it says, "Yea, though I walk." Here you have made the decision to walk through the valley of the shadow of death. The Lord did not lead you here. You made the decision to not follow his leading. But even though there are times you will not follow his leading, he will never leave you.

Thy rod and thy staff they comfort me.

His rod will beat down your enemies. His staff will comfort you.

Thou preparest a table before me in the presence of mine enemies.

In your walk with God, you will encounter many enemies such as troubles, lack, disease, addictions, or weaknesses. And right in the midst of your enemies, God will arrange, with great detail, a feast of provision for you, so your cup runs over and the world will see how good your God is.

Thou anointest my head with oil.

Sheep are especially troubled by the nose fly in the summer. These flies deposit their eggs in the sheep's nose where the eggs hatch and form into larvae. These larvae work their way up the nasal passages into the sheep's head. A good shepherd will put oil on the sheep's nose and head to keep these flies away. Flies are a picture of evil spirits. Oil is a picture of the Holy Spirit. The Holy Spirit teaches you truth to keep out the lies the evil spirits put in your head.

My cup runneth over.

The Lord does not just give you what you need. He gives you more than what you need. He does not just give you life. He gives you life more abundantly!

Surely goodness and mercy shall follow me all the days of my life.

The Lord's goodness and mercy will chase you down all the days of your life. The Hebrew word here for "follow" literally means chase you down!

And I will dwell in the house of the LORD for ever.

And you will dwell with the Lord forever! He lives inside of your spirit. He will never leave you!

What a beautiful picture of your walk through this life with your Lord. Meditate on Psalm 23 often to remind your soul to remain at rest, because your good Shepherd is taking great care of you.

Additional verses to meditate on:

"As for me, I will behold thy face in righteousness: I shall be satisfied, when I awake, with thy likeness." Psalm 17:15

"The Lord is my rock, and my fortress, and my deliverer; my God, my strength, in whom I will trust; my buckler, and the horn of my salvation, and my high tower." Psalm 18:2

"A merry heart doeth good like a medicine: but a broken spirit drieth the bones." Proverbs 17:22

"In righteousness shalt thou be established: thou shalt be far from oppression; for thou shalt not fear: and from terror; for it shall not come near thee." Isaiah 54:14

Chapter 5

SEEK GOD EVERY DAY

"O God, thou art my God; early will I seek thee: my soul thirsteth for thee, my flesh longeth for thee in a dry and thirsty land, where no water is; To see thy power and thy glory, so as I have seen thee in the sanctuary. Because thy lovingkindness is better than life, my lips shall praise thee. Thus will I bless thee while I live: I will lift up my hands in thy name. My soul shall be satisfied as with marrow and fatness; and my mouth shall praise thee with joyful lips: When I remember thee upon my bed, and meditate on thee in the night watches. Because thou hast been my help, therefore in the shadow of thy wings will I rejoice. My soul followeth hard after thee: thy right hand upholdeth me." Psalm 63:1-8

Not long ago I started getting up very early in the morning to spend time with God. One morning it did not happen, because I got up too late. As I was getting ready for work, I told God I will find some time to be alone with him today, and this is what he put on my heart: It will not be the same, because you will be distracted by people and all the things you have to get done today.

God was right. Our time together will not be the same during my busy day as it would have been in the morning when he would have had my total attention. God loves us so much. He wants our total attention so we can hear him and not be distracted. I will never look at my time spent with God in the same way again. I pray you will not either.

God wants you to seek him every day. He wants you to spend time with him. He wants you to talk to him. He wants you to ask him questions. He wants you to tell him what is bothering you. He wants you to leave all of your burdens with him. He wants you to thank him for his blessings. He wants you to praise him for who he is. I know most of us are so busy we cannot imagine finding time in our day for one more thing, but I want to encourage you to set aside at least ten minutes every day to seek God. Once you start noticing how much better your day flows because of the time you spent with God, you will increase the time you spend with him all on your own. Do what you can to make this time special between you and God. It will not take long before you will start looking forward to meeting God at that special time and place you have set aside just for him.

"As the hart panteth after the water brooks, so panteth my soul after thee, O God." Psalm 42:1

The time you set aside every day to spend with God will make all the difference in the world if you want to live a powerful, amazing, and victorious life. You will still talk to God and utter short prayers throughout your day or even cry out to God at times, but the time you set aside every day just to spend with God will be the most important part of your day. It is all about wanting to be in God's presence because he loves you. It is all about wanting to get to know him.

It is during this time you are spending with God that things start to happen in your life. It is during this time you have set aside for God that you will become best of friends. You reveal things to your best friend you would never reveal to anyone else. This is not just a one time or every once in a while thing. This is an every day thing saying to the Lord, "Here I am, Lord, talk to me about what you have for me today. Fill me with your love, so I can love others. Help me, Lord, with my problems. Give me wisdom and favor. Save my family. Accomplish your will for my life through me. Thank you for all your blessings, for they are many. I love you, Lord."

Different preachers call what is happening during this time different things, but it all leads to the same conclusion, God is working through your life. Some preachers call this the filling of the Holy Spirit. Some call this God's anointing. Some say it is God adding his super to your natural, so what comes out of you is supernatural, but it does not matter what you call it. What matters is you need this filling of the Holy Spirit, this anointing, this super added to your natural in order for God to work through you. You need this in order for Godly fruit to flow through your life. God working through you means no matter what happens throughout your day, God will respond through your spirit instead of you through your flesh, but this will not happen if you do not spend time with him every day. You need whatever he is giving during the time you are spending with him in order for him to work through you, otherwise you will be doing it all on your own (in the flesh).

"I am crucified with Christ: nevertheless I live; yet not I, but Christ liveth in me: and the life which I now live in the flesh I live by the faith of the Son of God, who loved me, and gave himself for me." Galatians 2:20

If you are seeking God every day by spending time with him and reading his Word, the Holy Spirit will speak to you. Listen for his voice in your spirit. Sometimes he will teach you something. Sometimes he will comfort you. Sometimes he will prompt you to do something or prompt you not to do something. Everything you are reading in this book is what God has taught me in the past few years through talking to him and reading his Word. This is how the Holy Spirit works inside of you.

"My sheep hear my voice, and I know them, and they follow me: And I give unto them eternal life; and they shall never perish, neither shall any man pluck them out of my hand. My Father, which gave them me, is greater than all;

and no man is able to pluck them out of my Father's hand. I and my Father are one." John 10:27-30

Seek God every day, because you cannot live a powerful, amazing, and victorious life apart from God. You have to let God live it through you. God lives his life through you by his Spirit. His Spirit guides you. God does not actually change you. Your flesh will always be flesh. When the Bible talks about your flesh, especially in the New Testament, it is talking about self effort. It is talking about the part of your soul that wants to get your needs met apart from God. The Bible says in Isaiah 64:6, that all of our righteousness is as filthy rags. It does not matter what good your flesh is trying to do, it can never please God.

Please get this truth, because if you keep trying to change yourself or do good yourself, you will be a miserable person. Every time you fail, you will feel like a miserable wretch and every time you succeed, you will have a tendency to look down on others who are not succeeding in that area. But when you realize it is not you, it is God living his life through you, then whatever is happening in your life, God gets all the glory. If you get a hold of this truth, it will set you free from working to please God or others. It will set you free from trying to change yourself. It will set you free to be who you are in Christ.

Additional verses to meditate on:

"But if from thence thou shalt seek the LORD thy God, thou shalt find him, if thou seek him with all thy heart and with all thy soul." Deuteronomy 4:29

"The Lord also will be a refuge for the oppressed, a refuge in times of trouble. And they that know thy name will put their trust in thee: for thou, Lord, hast not forsaken them that seek thee." Psalm 9:9-10

"But it is good for me to draw near to God: I have put my trust in the Lord God, that I may declare all thy works." Psalm 73:28

"Because he hath set his love upon me, therefore will I deliver him: I will set him on high, because he hath known my name. He shall call upon me, and I will answer him: I will be with him in trouble; I will deliver him, and honour him. With long life will I satisfy him, and shew him my salvation." Psalm 91:14-16

"Be careful for nothing; but in every thing by prayer and supplication with thanksgiving let your requests be made known unto God. And the peace of God, which passeth all understanding, shall keep your hearts and minds through Christ Jesus." Philippians 4:6-7

Chapter 6

STOP TRYING TO CHANGE YOURSELF

"Are ye so foolish? having begun in the Spirit, are ye now made perfect by the flesh?" Galatians 3:3

After I accepted Jesus Christ as my Savior in 1989, I started going to church every week. My biggest desire was to please God. The best way to do this, I thought, was to do what I heard in the sermons. Every time I heard a sermon about something I was doing that I should not be doing, I would make myself stop doing it. And every time I heard a sermon on something I should be doing that I was not doing, I would make myself do it. For example, after hearing a sermon about how I should not be listening to rock music, I went home and threw out all of my rock music. After hearing a sermon on why women should not wear pants, I went home and threw out all of my pants. I did not want to throw out my music or my pants, but I did it to please God.

After a few years of making changes like these in my life, I was miserable. Other changes I worked on were to be more loving, to be more patient, to be more peaceful, and to have more self control. The list of things I should not be doing or should be doing never ended. I was constantly working on myself by making myself do things or stop doing things. I was tired of wrestling with myself. I was worn out. So after about nine years of this, I quit going to church. I started listening to rock music again. I wore pants again. I stopped trying to change myself. It felt so good not to be wrestling with myself anymore. I was free. My soul was at rest again. When you stop trying to change yourself, all guilt will leave your soul. Guilt only comes when you fail at something. You cannot fail if you stop working on changing yourself.

I am not saying these changes I tried to make in my life were bad. What I am saying is I should not have tried to make these changes on my own, because even if I had succeeded in making these changes, it would have been by my flesh (self effort). I should have waited for the Holy Spirit to lead me. The difference is a man set goal versus a God inspired leading.

So what do you do if you should not try to change yourself? You walk with God. You let him lead you with his Spirit. When you accepted Jesus Christ as your Savior, not only did God's Spirit move inside of your spirit, Jesus' righteousness was put on you. There is nothing left for you to change. Jesus Christ redeemed your spirit, soul, and body, but your spirit is the only part that was saved immediately. That is why the Holy Spirit can live inside of your spirit, because it is completely saved and can never sin again. Your soul has been redeemed and will be saved after you die or at the rapture, whichever comes first and that is why you still sin even though you are saved, but remember even those sins have been paid for by Jesus. Your body is saved at the rapture where you will receive a new incorruptible body.

So what do you do with your soul which still sins, if you should not try to change it? First, believe what God says about you and your sins. God says you are righteous in his eyes and he will remember your sins no more. Believe this! Meditate on verses telling you who you are in Christ. Meditate on the verse about God removing your sins as far as the east is from the west. Meditate on God's love for you.

As you spend time talking to God and reading his Word, his Spirit will lead you. His Spirit will give you direction. You should never worry about changing yourself, because you have absolutely no power in your soul to fix that part of your life that you so desperately want fixed. It does not matter how much you try to change yourself, it will never be quite right. It does not matter how much you try to change yourself, it will never please God. Think of it this way, if you could be cleaned up by changing yourself, Jesus would not have had to die. Jesus did not die so you could be cleaned up. Jesus died because you could not be cleaned up. Jesus died so he could take your unclean and give you his clean.

A few weeks ago, I downloaded an app onto my iPhone called, MyFitnessPal. When I first logged onto the app, it asked me for my weight and how much I would like to lose in a week. Then it gave me a weekly calorie allowance in order for me to lose however many pounds I indicated that I wanted to lose in a week's time. I then entered the food I ate every day and it kept track of my daily calories. It also allowed me to enter any exercise I did, which basically added to my calorie allowance for that day. Instead of going on a diet and trying to change myself quickly, I just kept track of what I ate and let the app tell me the truth about what I ate (in calories) and the truth about exercising (the calories I burned). This truth changed the way I thought about the food I put in my mouth and about exercise.

Today, after reflecting on how much this app has changed my thinking, God put on my heart that the changes I am seeing in my thinking about food calories and exercise is much like how he wants me to see the changes in my thinking while daily walking with him. Instead of trying to change yourself, God wants you to read his Word (the truth) every day and spend time in prayer with him, and as you start keeping track of the truths you learn, your mind will start seeing things God's way. Your mind will start changing effortlessly. The Bible calls this renewing your mind.

So here is something you can do and should do. If you feel you need to be more patient, meditate on verses about patience. If you need more peace in your life, meditate on verses that talk about peace. Meditating on these verses will change your thinking. Once your thinking is changed, your body will follow. The sayings, "It's all in the mind," and "The battle is in the mind" are true. Change your mind and it will change your life. You change your mind by seeing the truth. My fitness app told me the truth about the calories in the food I was eating. The Bible tells you the truth about everything else.

The Bible is full of God's wisdom. All of your life you have been taught the world's way, but the world's way will only lead you down the path of destruction. You need to have a change of mind. You need to renew your mind. So read God's truth every day and you will effortlessly start seeing the changes you have always wanted to see, but this time they will stick because you first had a change of mind.

You will live a powerful, amazing, and victorious life by letting Christ live his life through you, not by changing yourself. As you walk daily with God, he will increase in your life and you will decrease which means more of God's character (fruit) will flow through your life and less of your old character (self effort) will flow through your life. And through all this, most of the things you think are wrong with you will just fall away without you having done anything except walk with God.

So stop judging yourself or trying to change yourself. Walk with God every day. Let him accomplish what he wants to accomplish through your life. Spend time with him and in his Word. Listen for his Spirit to guide you. Obey what he puts on your heart to do. In fact, every time you obey the Holy Spirit's leading, you are letting Christ live his life through you.

Additional verses to meditate on:

"For I will be merciful to their unrighteousness, and their sins and their iniquities will I remember no more." Hebrews 8:12

"For he hath made him to be sin for us, who knew no sin; that we might be made the righteousness of God in him." 2 Corinthians 5:21

"As far as the east is from the west, so far hath he removed our transgressions from us." Psalm 103:12

"And be not conformed to this world: but be ye transformed by the renewing of your mind, that ye may prove what is that good, and acceptable, and perfect, will of God." Romans 12:2

"I am crucified with Christ: nevertheless I live; yet not I, but Christ liveth in me: and the life which I now live in the flesh I live by the faith of the Son of God, who loved me, and gave himself for me." Galatians 2:20

Chapter 7

READ THE BIBLE

"The words of the Lord are pure words: as silver tried in a furnace of earth, purified seven times. Thou shalt keep them, O Lord, thou shalt preserve them from this generation for ever." Psalm 12:6-7

Pick a number. Ten, twenty, one hundred, one thousand, one million, any number. Let's say you picked 5,000. Now picture in your mind 5,000 Christians reading the same verses on the same day at the same time. Do you know every one of them will hear something different in their spirit, even though they are reading the same verses? This is why the Bible is like no other book in the world. The words in the Bible are alive. They can talk to your specific situation. God's power is behind every word written in the Bible. Every time you read the words in the Bible, God's power will accomplish whatever God wants them to accomplish in you. What you are hearing in your spirit while reading God's Word will depend on where you are in your walk with God. It will depend on what he is currently teaching you. It will depend on what questions you have asked him.

Behind every word in the Bible is God's voice. Everything written in the Bible is what God wants you to know about himself, about life on earth, and about eternal life. Never look to the Bible as a rule book. Always look for Jesus. In the book of John, it says Jesus is the Word, so when you spend time in God's Word, you are spending time with Jesus. You will not understand every word you read. That is okay. As you read the Bible, God's Spirit will reveal to you what he wants you to know. Focus on what you do understand. Take notes. Write down the verses that speak to you. God put his Spirit inside of you to teach you and to lead you. Listen for his voice as you read the Bible.

Read the Bible slowly. Think about what you are reading. Think about verses that stand out in your mind. Write down your thoughts. Ask God questions. Write down words you want to look up later. Never worry about how many chapters or verses you want to get through that day, because if you do, you will most likely hurry to get it done instead of taking your time to get something out of what you are reading. It is better to set a time limit for yourself, instead of a certain amount of verses or chapters you want to get through. Always look for Jesus when you are reading the Bible, because when you see him, you see yourself because you are in him. In 1 John 4:17, it says, as Jesus is, so are you right now in this world. As Jesus is, so are you in God's eyes.

Many Christians get frustrated because they do not understand what they are reading in the Bible. Only God understands everything written in his Word. He will reveal to you what he wants you to know. What you understand will be just what God wants you to understand, so do not get frustrated by what you do not understand. Each one of us has our own walk with God. New Christians have just begun their walk. Christians who have been saved for several years have been on this walk for awhile, but they still have a long way to go because this walk with God has no end. Yield yourself to him, to his leading, to his voice. Do not give it another thought if you do not understand everything you are reading. Read it anyway. As you spend time talking with God, ask him what you should read today. Ask him to lead you. I ask God all the time which book I should read next and every time I go to that book and start reading, I know it was for me because as I am reading, the words start to come alive for me.

You receive many spiritual benefits from reading the Bible, but did you know you also receive physical benefits? Reading God's

Word brings health to your body, peace to your soul, nourishment to your bones, and it add years to your life? So read it as often as possible. Study it as often as possible. Meditate on it as often as possible. Sing it as often as possible. You will be blessed every time you do!

Additional verses to meditate on:

"Thy word is a lamp unto my feet, and a light unto my path." Psalm 119:105

"My son, forget not my law; but let thine heart keep my commandments; for length of days, and long life, and peace, shall they add unto you. Be not wise in thine own eyes; fear the LORD, and depart from evil. It shall be health to thy navel, and marrow to thy bones." Proverbs 3:1-2, 7-8

"My son, attend to my words; incline thine ear unto my sayings. Let them not depart from thine eyes; keep them in the midst of thine heart. For they are life unto those that find them, and health to all their flesh." Proverbs 4:20-22

"For as the rain cometh down, and the snow from heaven, and returneth not thither, but watereth the earth, and maketh it bring forth and bud, that it may give seed to the sower, and bread to the eater: So shall my word be that goeth forth out of my mouth: it shall not return unto me void, but it shall accomplish that which I please, and it shall prosper in the thing whereto I sent it." Isaiah 55:10-11

"But he answered and said, It is written, Man shall not live by bread alone, but by every word that proceedeth out of the mouth of God." Matthew 4:4

Chapter 8

MEDITATE ON GOD'S WORD

"This book of the law shall not depart out of thy mouth; but thou shalt meditate therein day and night, that thou mayest observe to do according to all that is written therein: for then thou shalt make thy way prosperous, and then thou shalt have good success." Joshua 1:8

About ten years ago, I joined a type of speech club called Toastmasters. I was a member for about two years. I learned how to speak in front of an audience by giving speeches of all sorts. One day as I was thinking about the speeches I wrote during my time in Toastmasters, I was reminded of how happy I was all day long thinking about new speech titles or working on a particular speech. I wrote and gave 16 speeches while I was in Toastmasters. So for two years, I was always thinking on something to do with my next speech. As I was pondering this, this thought came to me, "Our mind needs something to meditate on."

While you are meditating on something, your mind is focused. While you are meditating on something, your mind does not wander. While you are meditating on something, bad thoughts cannot come in because they would only get in your way. When your mind is focused, it is harder to break into that. Here is another way to look at it. You are always thinking on something throughout your day. You are either thinking about a problem and how to fix it. Or you are thinking about something that happened in your past or an event in the future. Or you are thinking about what someone said to you.

Why not replace those thoughts with God's thoughts? His thoughts are truth. His thoughts bring life and health. Your thoughts often depress you. God's thoughts will have you soaring like an eagle above the storms of life. While you are meditating on verses about God's love, you are feeding on Jesus and tasting of his grace and mercy. In essence, you are filling yourself with Jesus and all that he is. And when you are filled with Jesus, what will come out of you effortlessly is the fruit of his Spirit. No wonder God says over and over again that we should meditate on his Word day and night.

There are many benefits from reading the Bible, but if you only read the Bible, you are only learning about the acts of God. If you want God to show you his ways, meditate on his Word. If you want God to give you revelation, meditate on his Word. Ask him questions about his Word. Look up words in Hebrew or Greek using a Strong's Concordance. Think about the verses you read during your day. Mull them over. Ponder them. Talk to God about them. Meditating on God's Word is much like a cow who chews the cud. A cow will chew on grass, swallow it, and then bring it back up again to chew on it some more. As you are meditating on a verse throughout your day, think about the words for awhile, then put them aside while doing other things, then bring them up to your mind again to think about them some more. All the while you are doing this, you will hear God's voice in your spirit revealing deeper truths about the words you are thinking about.

I recently read a book by John C. Maxwell called, <u>Thinking For A Change</u>. In this book, John Maxwell tells a story that really fascinated me. Here it is, more or less how I remember it. He said he was walking through the halls of a corporation when he looked in an office and saw a woman sitting in a chair looking out a window. He saw nothing else in the office. No desk. No computer. No trash can. Nothing, just a chair, a woman, and a window. When he asked why there was no desk or computer in this office, he was told that this woman gets paid to think. In fact, her last idea made them millions. Imagine that. Getting paid to think. Great ideas come from thinkers. Great revelations come from thinkers.

Just last night I was thinking about the words "victory in Christ" and "your victory is in Christ," but I could not put in words what they meant. While I was thinking about them, the Holy Spirit put this on my heart: Your victory is in Christ because every time you follow his leading, every time you do what he prompts you to do, you are heading toward victory in whatever area you need victory in.

I must tell you, you do not need to go to Bible school. The Holy Spirit is the best Bible School in the world. I have nothing against Bible School, but keep in mind that they will only teach you the acts of God. Only God can teach you his ways. Only God can give you revelation about his Word.

When you meditate on a verse, God will always give you revelation about that verse. To give you an example, I will share with you what God put on my heart when I meditated on 2 Corinthians 3:18, *"But we all, with open face beholding as in a glass the glory of the Lord, are changed into the same image from glory to glory, even as by the Spirit of the Lord."* After you get saved (under grace and not under the law anymore), while you are reading about the glory of the Lord in God's Word, believing in your heart that as he is, so are you in this world, meaning you are actually seeing yourself when you see Jesus, his Spirit transforms you into his image. It is you seeing you as Jesus is in God's eyes, no matter how you feel or what you see. That is what it takes for God's Spirit to transform you into the image of Christ.

What a revelation!!! What a truth!!! God's Word says the truth will set you free. Jesus is grace and truth. He will set you free from the law, from bondage, but that will only happen if you see yourself in this world AS HE IS. If you see yourself as you are, you will stay in bondage to the law, because you will continue to try to change yourself and you will, for the most part, fail. Even if you succeed at times, you will have a tendency to feel proud of what you have accomplished and may even turn your nose up to those who are failing at what you succeeded at. But most of the time you will fail and you will feel like a miserable wretch. Either way, that is not freedom. FREEDOM IS SEEING YOURSELF IN THIS WORLD, AS JESUS IS. Jesus is God's Beloved! Jesus is righteous! Jesus is beautiful! And so are you!

Psalm 1:1-3 says, *"Blessed is the man that walketh not in the counsel of the ungodly, nor standeth in the way of sinners, nor sitteth in the seat of the scornful. But his delight is in the law of the Lord ; and in his law doth he meditate day and night. And he shall be like a tree planted by the rivers of water, that bringeth forth his fruit in his season; his leaf also shall not wither; and whatsoever he doeth shall prosper."* When you meditate on God's Word, you are like a tree planted by living waters. God's fruit (love, joy, peace, longsuffering, gentleness, goodness, faith, meekness, temperance) will flow out of your life effortlessly. Your leaf (youth, health) will not wither. If you say, but I am meditating on God's Word, but I am still sick, then I say increase the dose! In Proverbs 4, it says his Word is health to all your flesh. In Hebrew, health here literally means medicine. You either need more medicine or stronger medicine, so keep meditating on God's Word. Especially meditate on verses about God's amazing grace, because that is the strongest medicine ever. You will bring forth fruit in due time!

As you are meditating on God's words throughout your day, you will find your soul will feel more at peace. You will find God's fruit flow out of your life effortlessly. You will find whatever you do, will prosper. Wisdom will be there when you need it. Healing will be flowing through your body. Your youth will be renewed. If you have God's Spirit in you and God's Word in your hand, you are the most blessed person in this world! You have access to all that Jesus has access to because his death gave you that access. You can come boldly to the throne and with confidence ask your Heavenly Father for anything. Thank you, Jesus!

Additional verses to meditate on:

"Open thou mine eyes, that I may behold wondrous things out of thy law."
Psalm 119:18

"For if the inheritance be of the law, it is no more of promise: but God gave it
to Abraham by promise. Wherefore then serveth the law? It was added because
of transgressions, till the seed should come to whom the promise was made;
and it was ordained by angels in the hand of a mediator. Galatians 3:18-19

"How sweet are thy words unto my taste! yea, sweeter than honey to my
mouth! Through thy precepts I get understanding: therefore I hate every false
way. Thy word is a lamp unto my feet, and a light unto my path." Psalm
119:103-105

"He made known his ways unto Moses, his acts unto the children of Israel."
Psalm 103:7

"All scripture is given by inspiration of God, and is profitable for doctrine,
for reproof, for correction, for instruction in righteousness.'" 2 Timothy 3:16

Chapter 9

MEDITATE ON GOD'S GRACE

"How excellent is thy lovingkindness, O God! therefore the children of men put their trust under the shadow of thy wings. They shall be abundantly satisfied with the fatness of thy house; and thou shalt make them drink of the river of thy pleasures. For with thee is the fountain of life: in thy light shall we see light." Psalm 36:7-9

I heard a preacher once say you get wisdom by meditating on God's Word. One day as I was pondering this, I told God this must not be true because I know of many people who meditate on God's Word but they are not making wise decisions. God then put on my heart the difference is what they are meditating on. You get wisdom from meditating on God's grace, not the law. You get wisdom from meditating on God's grace, not what is right or wrong. The law is all about what is right or wrong. God's grace is all about God's love and mercy. God's grace is all about Jesus.

In John 1:17, it says, *"For the law was given by Moses, but grace and truth came by Jesus Christ."* Truth is on the side of grace. It is truth that will set you free, not the law. When you read the Bible, what are you looking for? If you are looking for the law, you will find it. If you are looking for grace, you will find it. But honestly, do you really need more laws in your life? God just gave us the law, so we would know what sin is. God knew we could never keep his laws. Always come to the Bible looking for grace and you will find it in Jesus.

I want to share a testimony with you about the day I meditated on Jeremiah 9:23-24, *"Thus saith the LORD, Let not the wise man glory in his wisdom, neither let the mighty man glory in his might, let not the rich man glory in his riches: But let him that glorieth glory in this, that he understandeth and knoweth me, that I am the LORD which exercise lovingkindness, judgment, and righteousness, in the earth: for in these things I delight, saith the LORD."* This is a Scripture song, so I sang it to myself throughout the day. Each time I sang these verses, God gave me a different revelation concerning them.

After the first time I sang Jeremiah 9:23-24, I asked the Lord to help me understand him. I asked the Lord to help me get to know him better. Right after I said this, the Lord brought to my mind the last part of verse 24, *"for in these things I delight."* Then I looked at the words before *"for in these things I delight"* and saw, *"which exercise lovingkindness, judgment, and righteousness."* I then realized the Lord was telling me that he delights in lovingkindness, judgment, and righteousness.

The next time I sang Jeremiah 9:23-24, the Lord opened my eyes to the fact that the number one thing he delights in is lovingkindness, then judgment, then righteousness.

When I sang this Scripture song again, the Lord told me God exercised his judgment on the cross and the moment you believe this, the Lord's righteousness is imputed unto you. So now all that is left is the Lord's lovingkindness which he exercises every day in your life.

The last time I sang Jeremiah 9:23-24, the Lord told me he gives us wisdom, might (power and strength), and riches, but he does not want us to glory in what he gives us. He wants us to get to know him. He wants us to understand him, because everything we need is in him.

The next day as I was pondering on the Lord's lovingkindness, he brought to my mind some of my favorite verses, Psalm 103:1-5, *"Bless the LORD, O my soul: and all that is within me, bless his holy name. Bless the LORD, O my soul, and forget not all his benefits: Who forgiveth all thine iniquities; who healeth all thy diseases; Who redeemeth thy life from destruction; who crowneth thee with lovingkindness and tender mercies; Who satisfieth thy mouth with good things; so that thy youth is renewed like the eagle's."* And of course, the word "lovingkindness" jumped out at me. I believe what the Lord was telling me is to focus on his lovingkindness, because it is his lovingkindness (his grace) that gives us the power to overcome anything in our life that needs overcoming. Are you struggling? Are you hurting? Focus on the Lord's lovingkindness and not on your struggles or hurts, because while you are focusing on his lovingkindness, he is working on your struggles and hurts.

I want to share with you an entry from my journal dated January 26, 2014. This is what will happen in your life when you meditate on verses about God's grace.

"In the past few years my soul has come to completely trust God. In fact, my soul has totally let its guard down, because after several years of meditating on verses about God's grace and seeing his grace daily manifest in my life, my soul knows from experience that God is really that good. My soul has seen that God is good to me every day. My soul has seen that God has always lifted me up when I was down. My soul has learned to listen for God's voice in my spirit and follow it, because God's voice has always led me into victory. This is what resting in Jesus means. It means your soul is completely at rest, totally trusting that God's grace will show up in your life every day."

While you are meditating on God's grace, you will find yourself looking for it every day. The more you look for it, the more you will find it. A good place for you to start is to meditate on Psalm 103:1-5.

Additional verses to meditate on:

"Thou wilt shew me the path of life: in thy presence is fulness of joy; at thy right hand there are pleasures for evermore." Psalm 16:11

"Let them shout for joy, and be glad, that favour my righteous cause: yea, let them say continually, Let the Lord be magnified, which hath pleasure in the prosperity of his servant." Psalm 35:27

"Keep thy heart with all diligence; for out of it are the issues of life." Proverbs 4:23

"The fear of the Lord is the beginning of wisdom: and the knowledge of the holy is understanding." Proverbs 9:10

"How precious also are thy thoughts unto me, O God! how great is the sum of them! If I should count them, they are more in number than the sand: when I awake, I am still with thee." Psalm 139:17-18

Chapter 10

BE PATIENT WITH GOD, OTHERS, AND YOURSELF

Being confident of this very thing, that he which hath begun a good work in you will perform it until the day of Jesus Christ." Philippians 1:6

Be patient with God, others, and yourself. Every child of God has their own personal relationship with Jesus. There are no cookie cutter Christians. We are all unique. God has a different path for each of us. Some of you have just started your walk with God. Some of you have been walking with God for years. It is not for you to judge others. It is not for you to understand others. It is for you to walk with God down the path he has just for you.

I have always enjoyed reading self help books. Books about how to be a good mother, how to organize your house, how to be a good wife, diet books, and so forth. Many times, especially with diet books, I would set a day I would start, buy everything I needed, eat everything in the house the day before that was not on the diet, feel miserable the next day, eat something that made me feel better, and everything went downhill from there. Then I would beat myself up for not having the discipline to do what I was supposed to do. I would read the testimonials and think to myself if they can do it, so can I. But one day, God gave me a revelation. It was after another miserable diet failure, I was feeling extremely tired, bloated, mad at myself, and grumpy. I felt God saying to me, the problem is you are trying to work on all of your bad habits overnight. Changes like these come in small increments. God told me he works on us slowly, one thing at a time, otherwise we would become overwhelmed and quit. Change takes time because God first works on changing your mind.

One program I enjoy watching on television is Joyce Meyers' program called, "Enjoying Everyday Life." She said something on one of her programs that really jumped out at me about how long change in us can sometimes take. One day something became very clear to her. She was always angry with herself and others because things were not working out the way she thought they should. She often felt discouraged, upset, or feeling sorry for herself because of her past. For the first time in her life, she realized she was a miserable Christian and the devil was stealing her joy. She saw in the Bible that God wanted us to enjoy life, but she was miserable. That day she became angry with herself for not seeing this sooner, but also that day she purposed in her heart to change. Here is what struck me from what she said that day. She said it was eight or nine years later when she finally got complete victory over this. Eight or nine years later! That is how long it took God to work in her life to get her to enjoy her life and not get upset over her circumstances. Here is exactly what Joyce Meyer said in her own words:

> I remember when I realized that Jesus wanted me to enjoy my life and how the devil managed every day to steal that from me either through legalism or getting me upset about something or me feeling guilty about something. I didn't pray long enough. I didn't read the Bible enough. I wasn't sweet enough. I wasn't this. I wasn't that. Every single day of my life he found some way to steal my joy and I kept finding these scriptures that said Jesus died that we might have and enjoy life, and he wanted our joy to be full, ask and receive that your joy might be full, I've told you these things

that your joy might be full, and all of a sudden it hit me. That fire came in my belly. And I still remember where I was at in the house that we lived in, I was going up the steps to the second floor and I remember just stomping my feet and saying, 'You have stolen joy from me every day of my life and here I am at that time I was somewhere in my 40's and I thought I am not going to live like this anymore. I am going to get to the point where I enjoy every single day of my life. And you know, when I did, the war was on. Just because you make a decision doesn't mean the devil is going to go ooohhh. Oh, no, he'll come on full force, 'Oh, you think you are going to beat me. You think you are going to be free. Well, let me show you a few things.' So you better get really, really determined. And I had to study and study, and I had to learn what was stealing my joy. And I'll be honest with you, I'm not going to make any bones about it. It probably took maybe eight or nine years for me to realize all the different things the enemy used to steal my joy and to keep praying through it and studying and working through it and working through the emotions of it until I can pretty much say right now and I believe that my family would verify this. I would say that probably 99% of the time I enjoy my life. And if you knew how far I've come, but I remember that day on those steps when I made my mind up. Let me tell you something, a made up mind is a powerful thing. I mean you get a mind set in God's direction and the devil starts trembling. I made my mind up that I was going to have what Jesus died for me to have.

Be patient with God and give him time to work through you. If it were up to you, you would want to change yourself overnight, but it is not up to you. It is up to God. He created you with a free will and he wants you to choose him. He will not force you to do anything, but will patiently work with you to accomplish his will through your life.

Be patient with others, because God is working through them also. Are you praying for them? If you are, then you need to have faith God is answering. Believe his will will be accomplished in their lives. God deals with everyone differently. This is why you should never look at anybody else's life and wonder why God is dealing with them differently than he is dealing with you. God will not deal with you exactly the way he deals with anybody else. He will not deal with you in the exact timing that he deals with anybody else. God knows everything about you. He knows the way you are. He knows the things that have happened to you that have made you the way you are. God knows exactly what he is doing.

Be patient with yourself. God promised he will complete the work he started in you. Always keep your eyes on Jesus. Get direction from him. Keep your eyes off yourself.

Additional verses to meditate on:

"If it be possible, as much as lieth in you, live peaceably with all men." *Romans 12:18*

"Let us therefore follow after the things which make for peace, and things wherewith one may edify another." Romans 14:19

"As we have therefore opportunity, let us do good unto all men, especially unto them who are of the household of faith." Galatians 6:10

"Now we exhort you, brethren, warn them that are unruly, comfort the feebleminded, support the weak, be patient toward all men." 1 Thessalonians 5:14

"Great peace have they which love thy law: and nothing shall offend them." Psalm 119:165

Chapter 11

ALL THINGS WORK TOGETHER FOR GOOD

"And we know that all things work together for good to them that love God, to them who are the called according to his purpose." Romans 8:28

"Surely the wrath of man shall praise thee: the remainder of wrath shalt thou restrain." Psalm 76:10

In Romans 8:28, God promised he would work all things together for good. He would work it out, so everything that came into your life would be used for good. It does not matter if you did something on accident or if you did it on purpose, "all" is included in "all things." "All things" even include those things that came into your life you had absolutely no control over. In Psalm 76:10, God promised he would even use the evil deeds done to you for good, and whatever part of the evil he could not use for good, he would restrain. If you just stood on these two promises alone, you would have much peace in your soul.

One day as I was meditating on Romans 8:28, I noticed it said, "we know that all things work together for good." It did not say, "we know that all things work together for our good." I pondered this for a few months until one day, God spoke this to my heart. He said he did promise to work all things out for good, but sometimes it would not be for our good (at the moment), but for the good of others. In Isaiah 61:7, it tells us if the good was for others (instead of for us at the moment), he would repay us by giving us double for our trouble. *"For your shame ye shall have double; and for confusion they shall rejoice in their portion: therefore in their land they shall possess the double; everlasting joy shall be unto them." Isaiah 61:7*

God gave us the ultimate example of this in Joseph's life. God worked all things together in Joseph's life for the good of Israel and after thirteen years, Joseph received double for his trouble when he was elevated to second in command under Pharaoh. In Genesis 37-41, God tells us Joseph's story. He was sold into slavery by his own brothers. He ended up in prison for a crime he did not commit, but through it all God was with him. The Bible says Joseph was a goodly man and well favored. Wherever he went, he was favored in the eyes of those he served. Then one day, Joseph stood before Pharaoh and because God revealed to Joseph not only what Pharaoh dreamt, but also the meaning of those dreams, Pharaoh made Joseph second in command under him.

"And Joseph said unto his brethren, I am Joseph; doth my father yet live? And his brethren could not answer him; for they were troubled by his presence. And Joseph said unto his brethren, Come near to me, I pray you. And they came near. And he said, I am Joseph your brother, whom ye sold into Egypt. Now therefore be not grieved, nor angry with yourselves, that ye sold me hither, for God did send me before you to preserve life. For these two years hath the famine been in the land: and yet there are five years, in the which there shall neither be earing nor harvest. And God sent me before you to preserve you a posterity in the earth, and to save your lives by a great deliverance. So now it was not you that sent me hither, but God: and he hath made me a father to Pharaoh, and lord of all his house, and a ruler throughout all the land of Egypt." Genesis 45:3-8

God had a plan for Joseph's life and throughout all of his trials and tribulations, Joseph trusted God knowing God was with him.

But then Joseph's breakthrough came, and so will yours. Endure your problems with a good attitude. Ask God what he wants you to see. Ask God if there is anything you should be doing, but then go about enjoying your life. Trust God is working out his plan for your life and your breakthrough is just around the corner. Be ready, for you just might be standing in front of a Pharaoh one day.

Additional verses to meditate on:

"While we look not at the things which are seen, but at the things which are not seen: for the things which are seen are temporal; but the things which are not seen are eternal." 2 Corinthians 4:18

"John answered and said, A man can receive nothing, except it be given him from heaven." John 3:27

"Peace I leave with you, my peace I give unto you: not as the world giveth, give I unto you. Let not your heart be troubled, neither let it be afraid." John 14:27

"Wisdom is the principal thing; therefore get wisdom: and with all thy getting get understanding. Exalt her, and she shall promote thee: she shall bring thee to honour, when thou dost embrace her." Proverbs 4:7-8

"Wherein ye greatly rejoice, though now for a season, if need be, ye are in heaviness through manifold temptations: That the trial of your faith, being much more precious than of gold that perisheth, though it be tried with fire, might be found unto praise and honour and glory at the appearing of Jesus Christ." James 1:6-7

Chapter 12

SEE JESUS AS YOUR DAILY SAVIOR

"The righteous cry, and the Lord heareth, and delivereth them out of all their troubles. The Lord is nigh unto them that are of a broken heart; and saveth such as be of a contrite spirit." Psalm 34:17-18

Jesus not only wants to save you eternally, he wants to save you daily. He gets strength from saving you. Jesus wants to save you every day from temptation, from hurts, from troubles, from addictions, from whatever you have to deal with in your daily life. He wants to save you by giving you wisdom and strength. He wants to save you by fighting your battles for you.

My great niece, Lexi, who at the time was three years old, was sitting on a slide outside. She was too scared to slide down, and when she saw her Papa, she said to him, "Rescue me, Papa!" I just love this phrase! I think it makes our Heavenly Papa smile when we say, "Rescue me, Papa!"

In John 4:6-32, there is a story about Jesus resting by a well while his disciples went into town to buy food. While Jesus was resting, a Samaritan woman came up to the well to get water. After having a conversation with Jesus about his living water, she went into town to tell people about him. When Jesus' disciples returned, Jesus was joyful and looked refreshed. When they offered him food, he told them, *"I have meat to eat that ye know not of."* Jesus regained his strength after giving his living water to the Samaritan woman. Jesus met her need.

It gives him joy to meet your needs. He did not want anything from the woman at the well except to save her. He wants nothing from you except to save you. He wants you to come to him every day asking him to rescue you. He wants you to feed on him every day. Think about it. What do you have to offer Jesus? What can you give to Jesus? There is nothing good inside of you. Jesus cannot draw anything from you. He wants you to draw from him daily.

Always look to Jesus as your daily Savior. Never look to Jesus as your teacher or you will see him as someone giving you a set of teachings that you by your own effort must apply. Jesus did not come to be your teacher. Never look to Jesus as an example to follow, because his example will only condemn you by his perfect, sinless, holy life. Jesus came to this earth to be your Savior. Not a judge, not a lawgiver, but a Savior.

Additional verses to meditate on:

"The Lord shall fight for you, and ye shall hold your peace." Exodus 14:14

"The Lord also will be a refuge for the oppressed, a refuge in times of trouble. And they that know thy name will put their trust in thee: for thou, Lord, hast not forsaken them that seek thee." Psalm 9:9-10

"Now unto him that is able to do exceeding abundantly above all that we ask or think, according to the power that worketh in us, Unto him be glory in the church by Christ Jesus throughout all ages, world without end. Amen." Ephesians 3:20-21

"For by him were all things created, that are in heaven, and that are in earth, visible and invisible, whether they be thrones, or dominions, or principalities, or powers: all things were created by him, and for him: And he is before all things, and by him all things consist." Colossians 1:16-17

"Let us therefore come boldly unto the throne of grace, that we may obtain mercy, and find grace to help in time of need." Hebrews 4:16

Chapter 13

LISTEN FOR GOD'S VOICE

"My sheep hear my voice, and I know them, and they follow me." John 10:27

One day I was shopping for shirts to go with my new black pants. I had picked several shirts to try on. There was one plain white shirt I had picked, but right before I tried it on I felt something in my spirit telling me not to buy it. But I thought to myself as I was trying it on, "I can't imagine why not because it fits so nicely and looks great with my pants," so I bought it anyway. The following week I wore it to work. When I stood in front of the mirror in the restroom, I knew why I should not have bought the shirt. When I looked in the mirror, I noticed the shirt was slightly see through. I did not notice this in the dressing room, but here in the restroom at work with obviously different lighting, I noticed it. I knew right then it was God's voice telling me not to buy the shirt. I learned a valuable lesson that day. I need to learn to listen for God's voice in my spirit. I need to trust his guidance, even if I do not understand why at the time.

I remember some time after this shirt incident, I went to Barnes & Noble to buy a certain book. When I picked up the book, I felt something in my spirit telling me not to buy it, but I really wanted to read this book. It was a good spiritual book, so I thought. I bought it, but when I got home there was such a strong prompting in me to throw the book away, so even though I did not want to throw it away, I did because I knew without a doubt this time it was God prompting me to do this.

Eventually you will be able to discern between your voice and God's voice, but this takes time so be patient. In Hebrews 4:12, it says, *"For the word of God is quick, and powerful, and sharper than any twoedged sword, piercing even to the dividing asunder of soul and spirit, and of the joints and marrow, and is a discerner of the thoughts and intents of the heart."* This means reading God's Word will give you the sensitivity you need to discern your voice (soul) from God's voice (spirit).

Besides reading God's Word, something else that will help you discern God's voice in your spirit is having a clear conscience. In order to have a clear conscience, you must keep your mind off of your sins. In other words, do not be sin conscious. The Bible calls this "having an evil conscience," when your mind is always thinking about sin. An evil conscience is always accusing or excusing you or someone else of sin. God wants you to always be conscious of the righteousness you received from Jesus. God wants you to always be righteousness conscious. In other words, always keep in mind your right standing with God. It does not matter what you see, what you think, or how you feel. In God's eyes, you are righteous.

The day you accepted Jesus Christ as your Savior, he took your sin and gave you his righteousness. Jesus Christ never sinned. He did not deserve your sin, but he took it anyway. You were never righteous. You did not deserve his righteousness, but you received it anyway. Believe it. Accept it. Embrace it. It is a gift from your Heavenly Father. Always keep this on your mind and you will have a clear conscience.

There will come a time when you will not have a doubt that you are hearing God's voice in your spirit. There will come a time when you will obey his voice quickly, because you will have learned it is always to your advantage to obey quickly. I remember the day I knew without a doubt it was God's voice in my spirit and I obeyed quickly even though I did not want to, because I knew my victory was in my obedience to his voice. This one particular day I was not happy with one of my children. I could not wait to give them "a piece of my mind," but while I was thinking about what I was going to say, God's voice interjected. He asked me, what do you think it's going to do to them after you tell them that? I said, it will probably make them angry. Then God asked me, is that what you want to happen? I, of course, said, "no," because I knew God was telling me that giving my child "a piece of my mind" was not worth losing the peace in my home. Obey God's voice because his voice will always lead you to victory.

God's voice will speak to your spirit in many different ways, but more often than not, he sends thoughts to your mind (sometimes in whole paragraphs). Sometimes he just gives you a feeling. The best way to explain this is to say, "when in doubt, don't do it." That doubtful feeling is from the Holy Spirit. That doubtful feeling makes you lose God's peace in your spirit. Be led by God's peace. If you do not have peace in your heart about doing or saying something, then do not do it. When you allow God's voice to lead you, the Holy Spirit's fruit will effortlessly flow out of your life.

"But the fruit of the Spirit is love, joy, peace, longsuffering, gentleness, goodness, faith, Meekness, temperance: against such there is no law." Galatians 5:22-23

God's voice guides you with his counsel. Did you know God does not want you to make decisions by your conscience. He does not want you to be guided by your conscience. He wants you to be guided by his voice. He wants to guide you by his counsel. When God told Abraham to sacrifice his son, do you not think that violated Abraham's conscience? Of course, it did. But Abraham was led by God's voice, not by his conscience.

"Thou shalt guide me with thy counsel, and afterward receive me to glory." Psalm 73:24

Before I close this chapter, I want to remind you that the devil also puts thoughts into your mind. The Bible says we need to test the spirits and one way to do this, besides using God's Word, is to

55

consider how the thought makes you feel. If the thought makes you feel guilty and makes you want to run from God, then you know it is not from God. God convicts you of his righteousness, which makes you want to run to him for help. If the thought drives you, forces you, frightens you, confuses you, discourages you, worries you, condemns you, or manipulates you in any way, it is not from God. God gently leads and guides you by his Spirit. God's voice stills you, reassures you, enlightens you, encourages you, comforts you, and calms you. God is a Spirit and he speaks to you in your spirit, so use your spirit to discern the thoughts you receive. The Bible says God's Spirit bears witness with our spirit, meaning our spirit will know if it is God speaking to us. So do not think every thought you receive is from God. Use your spirit to discern the thought before you accept it as a thought from God.

Additional verses to meditate on:

"Howbeit when he, the Spirit of truth, is come, he will guide you into all truth: for he shall not speak of himself; but whatsoever he shall hear, that shall he speak: and he will shew you things to come. He shall glorify me: for he shall receive of mine, and shall shew it unto you." John 16:13-14

"For as many as are led by the Spirit of God, they are the sons of God." Romans 8:14

"But the wisdom that is from above is first pure, then peaceable, gentle, and easy to be intreated, full of mercy and good fruits, without partiality, and without hypocrisy." James 3:17

"Beloved, believe not every spirit, but try the spirits whether they are of God: because many false prophets are gone out into the world." 1 John 4:1

"The entrance of thy words giveth light; it giveth understanding unto the simple." Psalm 119:130

Chapter 14

WALK IN THE SPIRIT

"This I say then, Walk in the Spirit, and ye shall not fulfil the lust of the flesh. For the flesh lusteth against the Spirit, and the Spirit against the flesh: and these are contrary the one to the other: so that ye cannot do the things that ye would. But if ye be led of the Spirit, ye are not under the law." Galatians 5:16-18

When I woke up this morning, I asked God a question and as he sometimes does, he answered me right away. I have been struggling in an area of my life for some time now. I purposely will not tell you what it is because I want you to plug in your own thing you are struggling with. Sometimes I do good. Sometimes I don't do so good. I was doing so good last night, so I thought. Then it came across my path and I happily said yes, or more accurately, my flesh happily said yes again. So this morning, one of the first things I did was ask God, why did I say yes again? Why can't I just say no? This is what God said to me: It is because you are not walking in the Spirit.

It always amazes me how God teaches me what he is trying to get me to see. A lot of his teachings lately have been about worship and praise, and this morning when he said, it is because you are not walking in the Spirit, I knew in my heart what God said was the grand finale of what he was trying to get me to see. He wanted me to see when I am worshiping and praising Jesus, I am walking in the Spirit. While my mind is on Jesus and on his Word, I am walking in the Spirit.

Walking in the Spirit is walking in the knowledge that I am the righteousness of God in Christ. You walk in the Spirit by continually, from the moment you get up until you go to bed, think about your Savior and his goodness towards you. Yes, you have many things to do, but your many things to do will never give you the power to overcome what you need to overcome.

There is a story in Luke 10 about two sisters, Martha and Mary. When Jesus came to their house, Mary sat at the feet of Jesus listening to his every word. Martha was busy in the kitchen. When Martha got upset because Mary was not helping her, here is what Jesus said to her. *"Martha, Martha, thou art careful and troubled about many things: But one thing is needful: and Mary hath chosen that good part, which shall not be taken away from her."* You see, the many things you have to do are full of care and troubles, but spending time with Jesus is the good part.

Here is how you continually walk in the Spirit throughout your day. Start talking to Jesus the moment you get up in the morning. In between your daily work continue to talk to Jesus. Thank him for his goodness. Thank him for his many blessings. Praise him. Ask him questions. In fact, ask him lots of questions. He might not answer right away, but sometimes he does. You will love it. Tell him what is on your mind. Sing or hum hymns or Scripture songs. You can do this while you are walking to your car, walking to the restroom, going to lunch, cooking dinner, or making your bed. Whenever you find yourself alone, instead of talking to yourself or thinking about how upset someone made you or what you had for dinner last night, talk to Jesus. This is walking in the Spirit.

Always be aware of God's presence in your life. Keep your thinking focused on Jesus. If you are walking in the Spirit, you are being led by God's Spirit. You cannot be led by his Spirit if you are walking in the flesh. I suppose you can say that walking in the flesh is thinking about everything but Jesus. Walking in the Spirit means you are tuned into the spirit realm where you will easily be able to hear God's voice.

Additional verses to meditate on:

"Thou in thy mercy hast led forth the people which thou hast redeemed: thou hast guided them in thy strength unto thy holy habitation." *Exodus 15:13*

"Blessed be the Lord, who daily loadeth us with benefits, even the God of our salvation. Selah." *Psalm 68:19*

"But the Comforter, which is the Holy Ghost, whom the Father will send in my name, he shall teach you all things, and bring all things to your remembrance, whatsoever I have said unto you." *John 14:26*

"Every good gift and every perfect gift is from above, and cometh down from the Father of lights, with whom is no variableness, neither shadow of turning." *James 1:17*

"Trust in the LORD with all thine heart and lean not unto thine own understanding. In all thy ways acknowledge him, and he shall direct thy paths." *Proverbs 3:5-6*

Chapter 15

LET YOUR WORDS BE LIFE

"For verily I say unto you, That whosoever shall say unto this mountain, Be thou removed, and be thou cast into the sea; and shall not doubt in his heart, but shall believe that those things which he saith shall come to pass; he shall have whatsoever he saith. Therefore I say unto you, What things soever ye desire, when ye pray, believe that ye receive them, and ye shall have them."
Mark 11:23-24

Last December when my husband and I were driving our grandchildren to our house, our grandson, Jordan, who was 7 years old at the time, asked me if he could play outside when we got to our house. I told him, "No, you can't play outside today, because it is -20 degrees. You will freeze to death." Jordan then said to me, "No, I won't freeze to death." I, a little miffed, said to him, "People freeze to death every year and if you go outside today, you will also freeze to death." I will never forget the wisdom that came from my grandson's response to me. He said, "Don't say you will freeze to death, because that will go out into the universe and you will freeze to death. Say, I will not freeze to death and then that will go out into the universe and you will not freeze to death."

My grandson's response to me was full of wisdom and truth. In his own words he reminded me of what the Bible says in Proverbs 23:7, "As a man thinketh, so is he." Also, in Romans 4, the last part of verse 17 says, "God who quickeneth the dead and calleth those things which be not as though they were." The world calls this positive thinking. God calls this faith.

When you speak, you give life or death to whatever you are saying. Proverbs 18:21 says, *"Death and life are in the power of the tongue: and they that love it shall eat the fruit thereof."* God has given you the power to change your circumstances, and that power lies in your mouth.

Mark 11:23 says, *"For verily I say unto you, That whosoever shall say unto this mountain, Be thou removed, and be thou cast into the sea; and shall not doubt in his heart, but shall believe that those things which he saith shall come to pass; he shall have whatsoever he saith."* Notice it says *"saith"* three times and *"believe"* only once. God's words are seeds. You plant the seeds in your heart by speaking.

So start saying what you want to see, not what you see. Say what you want to have as if you already had it. Say, "The Lord is my Shepherd. I shall not lack. God shall supply all my needs according to his riches in glory by Christ Jesus," instead of, "I don't know where all my money goes. I never have enough money to last me through the month." I believe God will move mountains to make sure you have no lack.

Say, "Thank you, Jesus, for satisfying my mouth with good things, so that my youth is renewed like the eagles," instead of, "I am getting old. I feel so tired all the time."

Say, "Thank you, Jesus, for dying on the cross and bearing all of my infirmities. By your stripes I am healed and I receive your healing now," instead of, "I don't know what I am going to do. I have this constant pain in my knee." In fact, if you do have pain or sickness in your body, you can go even further with saying by commanding it in Jesus' name to leave your body and be cast into the middle of the sea.

If your child is a mess, do not talk to others about their messiness, instead say, "God, your Word declares that the seed of the righteous shall be delivered. Therefore, my children are delivered from every curse, every power of darkness and every evil. In the name of Jesus, I call forth a great, bright and blessed future for my children." When you speak positive words like this over your child, you are empowering them to succeed. But if you speak negative things like always talking about their messiness, you are actually empowering them to fail.

The key to receiving by faith is "saying." Many of you believe the right things about God's Word, but you are not saying them. Speak what you believe about God's Word, because when you speak, you are putting your faith into action. Believe God's Word, speak it, and you shall see it. Always choose life by speaking God's promises over your loved ones, over yourself, and over your situations. This will give you hope, build your faith, and change your circumstances as God's power is released.

Additional verses to meditate on:

"I will praise thee, O Lord, with my whole heart; I will shew forth all thy marvellous works. I will be glad and rejoice in thee: I will sing praise to thy name, O thou most High." Psalm 9:1-2

"Jesus answered and said unto them, Verily I say unto you, If ye have faith, and doubt not, ye shall not only do this which is done to the fig tree, but also if ye shall say unto this mountain, Be thou removed, and be thou cast into the sea; it shall be done." Matthew 21:21

"Finally, brethren, whatsoever things are true, whatsoever things are honest, whatsoever things are just, whatsoever things are pure, whatsoever things are lovely, whatsoever things are of good report; if there be any virtue, and if there be any praise, think on these things." Philippians 4:8

"Let no corrupt communication proceed out of your mouth, but that which is good to the use of edifying, that it may minister grace unto the hearers." Ephesians 4:29

"For this cause we also, since the day we heard it, do not cease to pray for you, and to desire that ye might be filled with the knowledge of his will in all wisdom and spiritual understanding." Colossians 1:9

Chapter 16

THE LORD'S PRAYER

After this manner therefore pray ye: Our Father which art in heaven, Hallowed be thy name. Thy kingdom come. Thy will be done in earth, as it is in heaven. Give us this day our daily bread. And forgive us our debts, as we forgive our debtors. And lead us not into temptation, but deliver us from evil: For thine is the kingdom, and the power, and the glory, for ever. Amen." Matthew 6:9-13

The Lord taught his disciples how to pray by saying this beautiful prayer in the book of Matthew. If you are like me, you probably have not said this prayer in awhile. One day while I was meditating on this prayer, I felt the Lord put this on my heart: Ask the Lord every day for your daily bread (your daily needs) and then trust he will provide them. Do not let the past bother you or the future worry you. Focus on today, because that is all God gives you. Let us go through this prayer together. In fact, why not meditate on it today.

Our Father
"And will be a Father unto you, and ye shall be my sons and daughters, saith the Lord Almighty." 2 Corinthians 6:18

Which art in heaven
"Unto thee lift I up mine eyes, O thou that dwellest in the heavens." Psalm 123:1

Hallowed be thy name

"And ye shall not swear by my name falsely, neither shalt thou profane the name of thy God. I am the Lord." Leviticus 19:12

Thy kingdom come

"And in the days of these kings shall the God of heaven set up a kingdom, which shall never be destroyed: and the kingdom shall not be left to other people, but it shall break in pieces and consume all these kingdoms, and it shall stand forever." Daniel 2:44

Thy will be done on earth

"And the world passeth away, and the lust thereof: but he that doeth the will of God abideth forever." 1 John 2:17

As it is in heaven

"The Lord has established his throne in heaven, and his kingdom rules over all." Psalm 103:19

Give us this day

"Therefore take no thought, saying, What shall we eat? Or, What shall we drink? or Wherewithal shall we be clothed? (For after all these things do the Gentiles seek:) for your heavenly Father knoweth that ye have need of all these things. But seek ye first the kingdom of God and his righteousness; and all these things shall be added unto you. Take therefore no thought for the things of itself. Sufficient unto the day is the evil thereof." Matthew 6:31-34

Our daily bread

"And Jesus said unto them, I am the bread of life: he that cometh to me shall never hunger; and he that believeth on me shall never thirst. John 6:35

Forgive us our debts

"Who forgiveth all thine iniquities; who healeth all thy diseases; Who redeemeth thy life from destruction; who crowneth thee with lovingkindness and tender mercies;" Psalm 103:3-4

As we forgive our debtors

"Then came Peter to him, and said, Lord, how oft shall my brother sin against me, and I forgive him? Till seven times? Jesus saith unto him, I say not unto thee, until seven times: but, until seventy times seven." Matthew 18:21-22

Lead us not into temptation

"Search me, O God, and know my heart; try me, and know my thoughts. And see if there be any wicked way in me, and lead me in the way everlasting." Psalm 139:23-24

But deliver us from evil

"But the Lord is faithful, who shall stablish you, and keep you from evil." 2 Thessalonians 3:3

For yours is the kingdom

"And the seventh angel sounded; and there were great voices in heaven, saying, The kingdoms of this world are become the kingdoms of our Lord and of his Christ; and he shall reign for ever and ever." Revelation 11:15

And the power

"He hath made the earth by his power, he hath established the world by his wisdom, and hath stretched out the heaven by his understanding." Jeremiah 51:15

And the glory

"Be thou exalted, O God, above the heavens; let thy glory be above all the earth." Psalm 57:11

Forever

"But the word of the Lord endureth for ever." 1 Peter 1:25(a)

Amen

"For all the promises of God in him are yea, and in him Amen, unto the glory of God by us." 2 Corinthians 1:20.

There is something you can do to take your prayer life to another level. Start your prayer with a song. The Bible says, *"Come before his presence with singing."* Then thank him for his blessings in your life. Praise him for who he is, your God, your Creator, your Father, your Shepherd, your Savior, your Provider, your Healer, your Comforter. *"Enter into his gates with thanksgiving and into his courts with praise."* After you are through thanking and praising him, your soul will be flying high above any storms in your life, even before you have asked God for anything.

Additional verses to meditate on:

"But thou, O Lord, art a shield for me; my glory, and the lifter up of mine head. I cried unto the Lord with my voice, and he heard me out of his holy hill. Selah. I laid me down and slept; I awaked; for the Lord sustained me. I will not be afraid of ten thousands of people, that have set themselves against me round about." Psalm 3:3-6

"Make a joyful noise unto the Lord, all ye lands. Serve the Lord with gladness: come before his presence with singing. Know ye that the Lord he is God: it is he that hath made us, and not we ourselves; we are his people, and the sheep of his pasture. Enter into his gates with thanksgiving, and into his courts with praise: be thankful unto him, and bless his name. For the Lord is good; his mercy is everlasting; and his truth endureth to all generations." Psalm 100:1-5

"Ask, and it shall be given you; seek, and ye shall find; knock, and it shall be opened unto you: For every one that asketh receiveth; and he that seeketh findeth; and to him that knocketh it shall be opened." Matthew 7:7-8

Chapter 17

FAITH WITHOUT WORKS IS DEAD

"What doth it profit, my brethren, though a man say he hath faith, and have not works? can faith save him? If a brother or sister be naked, and destitute of daily food, And one of you say unto them, Depart in peace, be ye warmed and filled; notwithstanding ye give them not those things which are needful to the body; what doth it profit? Even so faith, if it hath not works, is dead, being alone." James 2:14-17

I struggled for the longest time with James 2:14-17. I know we are saved by faith. I know faith is the only thing that pleases God. I also know there is nothing we can do physically (in our flesh) that pleases God, but my question was, "how can I reconcile these two?" How can faith without works be dead if our works do not please God? If faith is the only thing that pleases God, what is faith with works?

"But without faith it is impossible to please him: for he that cometh to God must believe that he is, and that he is a rewarder of them that diligently seek him." Hebrews 11:6

One day as I was talking to God about these verses, this is what he put on my heart: Faith is believing he is God. Works is the evidence that flows out of your life which reveals to the world that you have faith in God, but it is not your works, but God working through you. It is the Holy Spirit's fruit flowing out of you.

If you ask God for help with a situation and then go about your day worrying and wondering when God will answer, that is faith without works. But if you ask God for help and then go about your day rejoicing, believing in your heart that God is on it and he will answer in his time, that is faith with works. Believing that God is and living your life so the world knows you have faith in the living God. That is faith with works!

"Was not Abraham our father justified by works, when he had offered Isaac his son upon the altar? Seest thou how faith wrought with his works, and by works was faith made perfect? And the scripture was fulfilled which saith, Abraham believed God, and it was imputed unto him for righteousness: and he was called the Friend of God." James 2:21-23

Cast all of your cares upon God. Do not think about them anymore. Once you have asked God to do something about a situation, let it go. Stop thinking about it. There is tremendous power in letting go. The moment you let go and give it to God is the moment God starts moving. God moves when he sees faiths. That is faith with works.

Additional verses to meditate on:

"… for verily I say unto you, if ye have faith as a grain of mustard seed, ye shall say unto this mountain, remove hence to yonder place; and it shall remove; and nothing be impossible unto you." Matthew 17:20.

"And the scripture, foreseeing that God would justify the heathen through faith, preached before the gospel unto Abraham, saying, In thee shall all nations be blessed. So then they which be of faith are blessed with faithful Abraham." Galatians 3:8-9

"But that no man is justified by the law in the sight of God, it is evident: for, The just shall live by faith. And the law is not of faith: but, The man that doeth them shall live in them. Galatians 3:11-12

"Now faith is the substance of things hoped for, the evidence of things not seen." Hebrews 11:1

"But let him ask in faith, nothing wavering. For he that wavereth is like a wave of the sea driven with the wind and tossed. For let not that man think that he shall receive any thing of the Lord." James 1:6-7

Chapter 18

THE JOY OF THE LORD IS
YOUR STRENGTH

"Then he said unto them, Go your way, eat the fat, and drink the sweet, and send portions unto them for whom nothing is prepared: for this day is holy unto our Lord: neither be ye sorry; for the joy of the Lord is your strength." Nehemiah 8:10

In April of 2009, I flew to San Francisco for a conference. As soon as I got to my hotel room, I noticed I did not have my brown leather tote bag. I immediately went down to the front desk and looked to see if I left it by the front counter. When I did not see my tote bag on the floor, I asked the attendant at the front desk if anyone turned in a dark brown leather tote bag. She checked around her desk and even called the lost and found department, but the tote bag was nowhere to be found.

I went back to my room completely distraught. Not only was the tote bag worth about $200, my $300 camera was inside and also my Bible, and several books. I then got down on one knee and asked God to please bring my tote bag back to me. I also told him if I did not get it back, then I would accept it as his will for my life. This was a difficult thing for me to say to God, especially after I realized my $300 camera was also inside my tote bag. I then decided to do what

I had originally planned to do and that was to walk to town to do some shopping and eat dinner.

As I was walking to town I felt my heart getting heavy again with worry, so I started singing Scripture songs in my mind, and told myself whatever happens it is God's will for me. It really helps when you tell yourself the right things because if you do not, Satan will gladly tell you wrong things. Telling myself the right things and then singing Scripture songs totally took my mind off my tote bag and onto God and his promises. I had a wonderful evening of shopping and a nice dinner before I headed back to my hotel.

After I got back to my room, I called my husband and told him about my lost tote bag. He told me to ask the front desk if they had security cameras and if so, to ask them to check their cameras to see if I had left my tote bag by the front desk. I did this and the attendant told me to go back to my room and the security people would call me to let me know if they saw anything. About two minutes after I got to my room, the front desk called me and said they had my tote bag. Apparently, I had left my tote bag in my taxi, the taxi driver brought it to the security station, and they had it all along.

After much reflection on this whole incident, I believe this was a test from God. I remembered when I was deciding what to carry in my tote bag, I felt God put on my heart not to take my 20 year old, precious to my soul, Bible, but to take the Bible I had just recently bought. He also put on my heart not to take my to do/calendar book with me which contained a lot of personal information. I believe in my heart God knew if my tote bag contained those two items, I would have been too distraught to learn the lesson he wanted me to learn. That day I was thankful for God's promise that he would not put on us more than we can handle.

"There hath no temptation taken you but such as is common to man: But God is faithful, who will not suffer you to be tempted above that ye are able: but will with the temptation also make a way to escape, that ye may be able to bear it." 1 Corinthians 10:13

Do not lose your strength because you are the joy of the Lord. Do not let people or circumstances steal your strength, because you are the joy of the Lord. Do not let the devil steal your strength, because you are the joy of the Lord. If you feel your strength slipping away like I did, encourage yourself in the Lord by singing Scriptures songs or hymns, by listening to worship songs, by reading his Word, by praising him. Remind yourself you are a child of the Most High God and you are going to live eternally with him. Remind yourself of how good and merciful God is to you every day. Remind yourself Jesus loves you. You are his joy! After a little while, you will feel your strength coming back. Remember the devil does not want your material things. He wants your strength. He wants your peace. If he can upset you and get your mind off of God, he has won. If the devil can get you to look at your circumstances instead of looking at Jesus, he has won. Do not let anything steal your strength, because you are the joy of the Lord and this revelation will give you strength.

Additional verses to meditate on:

"The thief cometh not, but for to steal, and to kill, and to destroy. I am come that they might have life, and that they might have it more abundantly." *John 10:10*

"Now the God of hope fill you with all joy and peace in believing, that ye may abound in hope, through the power of the Holy Ghost." *Romans 15:13*

"I can do all things through Christ which strengtheneth me." *Philippians 4:13*

"My brethren, count it all joy when ye fall into divers temptations; Knowing this, that the trying of your faith worketh patience." *James 1:2-3*

"Whom having not seen, ye love; in whom, though now ye see him not, yet believing, ye rejoice with joy unspeakable and full of glory: Receiving the end of your faith, even the salvation of your souls." *1 Peter 1:8-9*

Chapter 19

LABOR TO ENTER INTO HIS REST

"There remaineth therefore a rest to the people of God. For he that is entered into his rest, he also hath ceased from his own works, as God did from his. Let us labour therefore to enter into that rest, lest any man fall after the same example of unbelief." Hebrews 4:9-11

There will always be a struggle between the holy you and the human you, like twins struggling in the womb. You might pray, "let the holy one kill the human one," but that is not going to happen. And the devil may pray, "let the human one kill the holy one," but grace says, that is not going to happen. So you live with twins struggling in your womb. This is where your labor begins. Labor to enter into his rest.

I used to have a hard time controlling my emotions. Do you have that problem? Even though I would pray about what was troubling me, I would still worry. I would worry about how God would respond, when he would respond, or even if he would respond. I read verses in the Bible like, *"Wait on the Lord and be of good courage, and he will strengthen your heart,"* but I did not know how to just wait without doing something, thinking something, or saying something about what was troubling me. Then God took me on a journey which helped me tremendously. I would like to take you on this journey. This journey changed my whole perspective on what it means to labor to enter into his rest. So sit back, relax, and enjoy this journey with me.

About 2,000 years ago, Jesus Christ laid down his life on a cross to pay for the sins of the whole world. Right before he died, he said, *"It is finished."* His work was done. He was now able to stop working and rest. In fact, as soon as Jesus Christ returned to heaven, he sat down at the right hand of the Father. Jesus is now resting, because his work is done. Jesus Christ is now resting in heaven next to his Father, waiting for the Father to tell him it is time to get his bride (the church).

Now picture this in your mind. You just realized who Jesus Christ was. You just realized why Jesus Christ came to this earth. You then accepted him as your Savior. You have never felt so loved. You have never felt so free. All of your guilt fell away. You are now saved eternally to live forever with Jesus Christ! What a glorious day it is! All of heaven rejoiced because of you. All of heaven rejoiced with you. But here is what you did not see, but what heaven saw. The moment you accepted Jesus Christ as your Savior, that very moment you were put into Christ. You are now seated IN CHRIST in heaven next to the Father. You are as loved by the Father as Jesus is. Rest, love, joy, and peace are yours in Christ. Victory for every one of your battles is in Christ. You are surrounded by God's favor in Christ. All of God's blessings are yours in Christ. In fact, everything you will ever need, want, or desire is in Christ. Are you jumping for joy yet?

Now picture this in your mind. Something has just upset you. It is troubling you. It is making you worry. Your soul has become restless. You did not see it, but all of heaven did. The moment your soul became restless, you stood up. The moment you stood up, you got out of CHRIST. The moment you got out of Christ, you stopped trusting him. You are now trusting in yourself to come up with a solution.

Now you must be thinking how do you not worry or let something trouble you? As soon as something starts to trouble you, get alone with Jesus and talk to him. Ask him to give you wisdom of what to say or do. Tell him you are not going to worry, because you are trusting in him. Thank him for his wisdom. Thank him for his blessings. Thank him for loving you. After you are done talking to Jesus, your soul should have calmed down. If not, read the Bible, especially verses about God's grace. Psalm 23 and Psalm 103:1-5 are excellent for this. Sing hymns or Scripture dongs. Stay with Jesus and in his Word until your soul sits back down in him.

In Hebrews 4, it says when you enter into Christ's rest, you ceased from your own works. This does not mean you stop working physically. It means you stop working mentally. It means you stop worrying and wondering. It means you stop striving to make things work. It means you stop trying to figure it all out. You rest in Christ trusting he will take care of you. You enjoy being in his presence. If you need something, tell him, but do not let your soul become restless. If you are hurting, tell him. When you hold onto your cares, you are doubting God. You are saying to God, "I have to hold onto these cares, because I do not trust that you will take care of them." Your labor should not be to hold onto your cares. Your labor should be to enter into the Lord's rest where you do not have any cares, because you have given them all to the Lord.

Be still, and know that I am God." Psalm 46:10(a)

Entering into Christ's rest and ceasing from your own works will bring much peace to your soul. Peace in your soul does not just happen. You have to aggressively pursue it. If you are a child of God and something does not work out the way you had planned, do not get upset. Do not get restless. Remember God is directing your steps. He probably did not want you to go there, or say that, or watch that, or read that. Just go with it, because if God wanted it to happen in your life, it would have happened. Tell yourself that nothing comes into your life without God's permission. Tell yourself whatever God allows in your life, he will work out for good. What the devil means for harm, God intends for good. Remain at peace. Talk to Jesus about it, but do not get restless.

Always keep your mind on Jesus. A mind stayed on Jesus talks to him throughout the day. A mind stayed on Jesus always listens for his voice. A mind stayed on Jesus meditates on his Word throughout the day. A mind stayed on Jesus stays in his rest.

Additional verses to meditate on:

"But let all those that put their trust in thee rejoice: let them ever shout for joy, because thou defendest them: let them also that love thy name be joyful in thee. For thou, Lord, wilt bless the righteous; with favour wilt thou compass him as with a shield." Psalm 5:11-12

"O how love I thy law! it is my meditation all the day. Thou through thy commandments hast made me wiser than mine enemies: for they are ever with me. I have more understanding than all my teachers: for thy testimonies are my meditation." Psalm 119:97-99

"Thou wilt keep him in perfect peace, whose mind is stayed on thee: because he trusteth in thee." Isaiah 26:3

"When the even was come, they brought unto him many that were possessed with devils: and he cast out the spirits with his word, and healed all that were sick: That it might be fulfilled which was spoken by Esaias the prophet, saying, Himself took our infirmities, and bare our sicknesses." Matthew 8:16-17

"Come unto me, all ye that labour and are heavy laden, and I will give you rest. Take my yoke upon you, and learn of me; for I am meek and lowly in heart: and ye shall find rest unto your souls. For my yoke is easy, and my burden is light." Matthew 11:28-30

Chapter 20

PRAISE THE LORD FOR THE BATTLE IS THE LORD'S

"And he said, Hearken ye, all Judah, and ye inhabitants of Jerusalem, and thou king Jehoshaphat, Thus saith the Lord unto you, Be not afraid nor dismayed by reason of this great multitude; for the battle is not yours, but God's." 2 Chronicles 20:15

In 2 Chronicles 20, there is a story about a king, which gives us the answer on how to handle every battle in our lives. It does not matter who or what you are battling. It could be a change you want to see happen in your life. It could be an addiction. It could be your circumstances. It could be a weakness in yourself that you do not like. It does not matter what battle you are fighting in your soul, it is not your battle. It is the Lord's battle. And since it is the Lord's battle, go to him immediately to get directions on how you should respond. Remind the Lord of his promises from his Word. This is what King Jehoshaphat did the day he received a message that a great multitude of Moabites and Ammonites were coming to do battle with him. The Bible says, *"Jehoshaphat feared, and set himself to seek The Lord, and proclaimed a fast throughout all Judah."* All the people of Judah came together to ask the Lord for help. Before all the people of Judah, King Jehoshaphat prayed this prayer, *"O Lord God of our fathers, art not thou God in heaven? and rulest not thou over all the kingdoms of the heathen? and in thine hand is there not power and might, so that none is able to withstand thee? Art not thou our God, who didst drive out the inhabitants of this land before thy people Israel, and gavest it to the seed of Abraham thy friend for ever? And they dwelt therein, and have built thee a sanctuary therein for thy name, saying, If, when evil cometh upon us, as the sword, judgment, or pestilence, or famine, we stand before this house, and in thy presence, (for thy name is in this house,) and cry unto thee in our affliction, then thou wilt hear and help. And now, behold, the children of Ammon and Moab and mount Seir, whom thou wouldest not let Israel invade, when they came out of the land of Egypt, but they turned from them, and destroyed them not; Behold, I say, how they reward us, to come to cast us out of thy possession, which thou hast given us to inherit. O our God, wilt thou not judge them? for we have no might against this great company that cometh against us; neither know we what to do: but our eyes are upon thee."*

After the king's prayer, the Spirit of God spoke through Jahaziel, and he said, *"Hearken ye, all Judah, and ye inhabitants of Jerusalem, and thou king Jehoshaphat, Thus saith the Lord unto you, Be not afraid nor dismayed by reason of this great multitude; for the battle is not yours, but God's. To morrow go ye down against them: behold, they come up by the cliff of Ziz; and ye shall find them at the end of the brook, before the wilderness of Jeruel. Ye shall not need to fight in this battle: set yourselves, stand ye still, and see the salvation of the Lord with you, O Judah and Jerusalem: fear not, nor be dismayed; to morrow go out against them: for the Lord will be with you."* After God spoke through Jabaziel, the king and the people worshipped the Lord.

The next morning King Jehoshaphat said to the people, *"Hear me, O Judah, and ye inhabitants of Jerusalem; Believe in the Lord your God, so shall ye be established; believe his prophets, so shall ye prosper."* Then the king appointed singers who went out before the army singing, *"Praise the Lord, for his mercy endureth for ever."* And the Bible says, *"And when they began to sing and to praise, the Lord set ambushments against the children of Ammon, Moab, and mount Seir, which were come against Judah; and they were smitten."* Everyone of Judah's enemies that came to do battle with them were dead. Not one of their enemies escaped. Not one of your enemies will escape if you let the Lord fight your battles. Your enemies today are no longer people, but instead anything that takes you out of resting in Christ: troubles, lack, disease, addictions, or weaknesses. If you let the Lord fight your battles, all of your enemies will be put to death.

I have a son who I always worried about. I use to pray for him every day asking God for certain things to happen in his life. I prayed the same things for him over and over again for years and saw little change, until one day I said this to God, "I don't understand. Is this what I should be doing, praying for the same things over and over again, because I am getting tired of praying and nothing is happening? Am I not seeing something? Am I doing something wrong?" And this is what God put on my heart: Just start thanking me for the things you are praying for. So that is what I did from that day on. Instead of praying for what I would like to see in my son's life, I thanked God for those very things in my son's life, even though I saw no evidence of it.

One of things I was thanking God for is a job for my son. My son has disabilities, which makes it hard for him to stay on a job. About one month after thanking God for a job for my son, a corporation who only hires people with disabilities got the bid at a military base near us to take care of their dining facilities. My son not only got a job with them, but he is now a shift leader!

Ever since the day I had that conversation with God about my son, I have not worried about him or his job or anything about his life. In fact, every time worry tries to creep in, I immediately thank God for taking care of my son and the worry flees. The day I started thanking God for taking care of my son is the day I stopped fighting this battle. It is the day I stopped struggling and rested. That very day God took over and won this battle for me.

The battle is the Lord's, so focus on the Lord and not on your troubles, lack, disease, addictions, or weaknesses. What you focus on in your life becomes bigger, so the more you focus on the things you are battling, the bigger your battle will become. Give all of your battles to the Lord. Focus only on him. Spend time with the Lord. Get to know him. Get to know how much he loves you. Thank him for his goodness and mercy. The more you get to know the Lord, the bigger he becomes in your life.

Additional verses to meditate on:

"The LORD shall fight for you, and ye shall hold your peace." Exodus 14:14

"And all this assembly shall know that the LORD saveth not with sword and spear: for the battle is the LORD's, and he will give you into our hands." 1 Samuel 17:47

"For the eyes of the LORD run to and fro throughout the whole earth, to shew himself strong in the behalf of them whose heart is perfect toward him." 2 Chronicles 16:9(a)

"For ever, O Lord, thy word is settled in heaven. Thy faithfulness is unto all generations: thou hast established the earth, and it abideth." Psalm 119:89-90

"As ye have therefore received Christ Jesus the Lord, so walk ye in him: Rooted and built up in him, and stablished in the faith, as ye have been taught, abounding therein with thanksgiving." Colossians 2:6-7

Chapter 21

MEET GOD IN HIS SECRET PLACE

"Make a joyful noise unto the Lord, all ye lands. Serve the Lord with gladness: come before his presence with singing. Know ye that the Lord he is God: it is he that hath made us, and not we ourselves; we are his people, and the sheep of his pasture. Enter into his gates with thanksgiving, and into his courts with praise: be thankful unto him, and bless his name. For the Lord is good; his mercy is everlasting; and his truth endureth to all generations."
Psalm 100:1-5

There is a spiritual place where you can go where you can almost feel God's presence. Psalm 91:1 calls it the secret place of the most High. *"He that dwelleth in the secret place of the most High shall abide under the shadow of the Almighty."* It is not a physical place. It is a spiritual place. It is a place where you are in the presence of God spiritually. It is a place where God totally fills you with his Spirit.

In Psalm 100, King David gives us three keys that will get us into God's secret place: SINGING, THANKSGIVING, AND PRAISE. *"Come before his presence with singing."* Always start your prayer by singing to the Lord. Sing a Scripture song. Sing a hymn. Sing a worship song. Nothing will prepare your heart for prayer like singing to your Savior about his goodness. *"Enter his gates with thanksgiving."* You have so much to be thankful for. Thank Jesus for all he has done for you. Thank him for saving you. Thank him for his faithfulness. Thank him for his love. Thank him for his provision. Thank him for his goodness. While you are thanking Jesus, you are entering into his gates. You are on your way to God's secret place.

"Enter into his courts with praise." Praise is declaring the truth of the Lord, sometimes before you see it manifested in your life. It is speaking in faith what the Lord has promised you. It is giving him honor. It is telling him you trust him. Every time you stand on a promise from God, the devil will immediately try to create the opposite in your life through circumstances. He does this to get you to doubt God's promise. When this happens, you have two options. You choose to believe and proclaim the promise of God or you choose to believe the circumstances the devil created. What you believe and proclaim will determine what your future will be. It is not always easy to look beyond your circumstances, but you need to hold onto what God has promised you. It starts with a decision of your will, followed by your proclamation. Your proclamation of God's promises become praises. With praises you celebrate and proclaim everything God did. You celebrate and proclaim everything he promised he would do.

"But thou art holy, O thou that inhabitest the praises of Israel." Psalm 22:3

Once you are in God's secret place, offer yourself to him. Give him all of you. By doing this, you are left empty handed, but you will not leave empty handed. After you are finished telling God everything you want to tell him, be still for awhile and wait. It is in this silence that he will speak to you. God wants you to get to know him. He wants to reveal his ways to you. No one will know what he says to you except you. That is why it is called the secret place.

Additional verses to meditate on:

"The secret things belong unto the Lord our God: but those things which are revealed belong unto us and to our children for ever, that we may do all the words of this law." Deuteronomy 29:29

"In every thing give thanks: for this is the will of God in Christ Jesus concerning you." 1 Thessalonians 5:18

"Thou wilt shew me the path of life: in thy presence is fulness of joy; at thy right hand there are pleasures for evermore." Psalm 16:12

"Oh that men would praise the Lord for his goodness, and for his wonderful works to the children of men! And let them sacrifice the sacrifices of thanksgiving, and declare his works with rejoicing." Psalm 107:21-22

"And be not drunk with wine, wherein is excess; but be filled with the Spirit." Ephesians 5:18

Chapter 22

YOU ARE NEVER TOO OLD TO START SERVING GOD

"And Enoch lived sixty and five years, and begat Methuselah: And Enoch walked with God after he begat Methuselah three hundred years, and begat sons and daughters. And all the days of Enoch were three hundred and sixty and five years." Genesis 5:21-24

One day as I was pondering how old I was, 46 at the time, I thought to myself how I wished I had learned all that God was teaching me now when I was younger. I thought to myself, "I could have given so much more of my life to God if only I had started younger." God immediately interjected. He told me age does not matter to him. He will work through whoever will let him. That morning I read in Genesis about Enoch. Enoch lived 365 years but he did not start walking with God until he was 65 years old. It does not matter how old you are. God has a plan for your life. If you seek him, he will reveal his plan to you. If you will let him, God will use your life to turn this world upside down for Jesus!

It was about a year ago, in the month of May, I was almost through with my first class at Faith Bible Institute. I decided to write my Pastor an email thanking him for bringing Faith Bible Institute to our church. I also shared with him how much I was learning and what God was doing in my life. I remember it was a Friday evening. The next morning I checked my email and saw my Pastor had responded. He was encouraged to hear what God was doing in my life. He said he would really like it if I could share this with the congregation during testimony time one Sunday evening. While I was getting ready to run my errands that morning, I was talking to God about how I should respond to my Pastor. I was not able to come to the Sunday night service and did not foresee this happening for some time. While I was talking to God about this, I clearly heard God say to me, "You are not going to just tell the Sunday night service, you are going to tell the world. You are going to write a book." I could not believe what I had just heard, but I was excited because I often told God how I wanted to shout from the rooftops what he was doing in my life. Right after God told me this, thoughts started flooding my mind. I sat down with a pen and paper and could not write fast enough of what God was bringing to my mind. God gave me the title of the book, <u>My Journey With God</u>, all the chapter titles and much of the content. After the weekend was over, I had twenty typed pages of my first book. As I reflect on this years later, I believe God gave me this message in exactly this way, because every time I would doubt God had told me this, I would remember that Saturday morning and think to myself, there is no way that I made this up. I am not a writer. I have never wanted to write anything, much less a book. I believe it was my "burning bush," so to speak. No one could tell me that this was not from God. My Pastor often says, "Don't doubt in darkness what God made clear to you in the light."

You are never too young or too old to serve God. Seek him and you will find him. Let him lead you. Let him love you. Let him teach you. Let him provide for you. Let him comfort you. You will learn, as I did, if you have Jesus, you have everything you need in life.

Additional verses to meditate on:

"Now also when I am old and grayheaded, O God, forsake me not; until I have shewed thy strength unto this generation, and thy power to every one that is to come." Psalm 71:18

"It is a good thing to give thanks unto the Lord, and to sing praises unto thy name, O most High: To shew forth thy lovingkindness in the morning, and thy faithfulness every night." Psalm 92:1-2

"For I know the thoughts that I think toward you, saith the Lord, thoughts of peace, and not of evil, to give you an expected end." Jeremiah 29:11

"And ye shall seek me, and find me, when ye shall search for me with all your heart." Jeremiah 29:13

"I am the vine, ye are the branches; He that abideth in me, and I in him, the same bringeth forth much fruit; for without me ye can do nothing." John 15:5

Chapter 23

YOUR ENEMY IS THE DEVIL, NOT PEOPLE

"Put on the whole armour of God, that ye may be able to stand against the wiles of the devil. For we wrestle not against flesh and blood, but against principalities, against powers, against the rulers of the darkness of this world, against spiritual wickedness in high places." Ephesians 6:11-12

Your enemy is the devil, not people, but with that said, the devil will almost always use people to get to you. He does this by putting thoughts into people's minds. The Bible calls these thoughts from the devil "fiery darts." This is why it is so important for you to watch what you are thinking about. Do not just accept every thought that comes into your mind. The Bible tells you to take every thought captive for this reason. If whatever you are thinking about is depressing you, upsetting you, or you are thinking bad thoughts about someone, stop and remember these thoughts are coming from the devil. Do what Jesus did when he was tempted of the devil in the wilderness, tell him what God's Word says about his lies.

Jesus is 100% man and 100% God. When the devil spoke to Jesus in the wilderness, the devil spoke to the man in Jesus. The man who has a mind, emotions, and a will. And that is the same way the devil will come to you every time. He will appeal to the man in you. But learn from Jesus by how he responded to the devil. Jesus always responded by saying, "It is written," and that is the same way you should respond every time the devil speaks a lie to your mind. The Bible says the devil is the father of lies, so everything he says will be a lie. Always respond to the devil by saying, "It is written." Speak out loud the Bible verses that come to your mind, and the devil will flee.

Another name the Bible calls the devil is the accuser of the brethren, because many of the "fiery darts" he shoots into your mind will be accusations. The devil will condemn you or more accurately, get you to condemn yourself or someone else. Every time you fail, the devil will tell you God no longer loves you. He will tell you that you will never measure up. He will tell you that you will never be good enough for God. These are ALL lies.

If you fail and feel condemned, remember after you are saved, condemnation of sin comes only from the devil. But here is something that will help you. The devil can only condemn you if you are sin conscious, but he cannot condemn you or accuse you if you are righteousness conscious. Being righteousness conscious means you are always conscious of your right standing with God because of Jesus. It is much like the law. When you were under the law, the law condemned you by showing you that you have transgressed (broke) the law, but now that you are under grace, nothing can condemn you because grace is God's unmerited, unearned, undeserved favor of God on your life.

After you got saved, Jesus took your sin and gave you his righteousness. You should always be conscious of your righteousness in Christ. You should always be conscious of your right standing with God. You should no longer be conscious of your sins. God said he will remember your sins no more and neither should you.

Every time you fail, God's grace will pick you up and convict (remind) you of your righteousness in Christ. How do you tell the difference between condemnation and conviction? Condemnation pushes you away from God. Conviction draws you towards God. Condemnation says, "Run because there is no answer." Conviction says, "There is an answer." Condemnation says, "You might as well run away from God because he will not understand." Conviction says, "Come unto me all you that labor and are heavy laden and I will give you rest. Cast your care upon me because I care for you."

Always remember God loves you unconditionally. He loves you with reckless extravagance. Remind yourself that Jesus was condemned in your place. It is finished! Jesus paid it all! God will never condemn you again. God now works with you every day, teaching you, guiding you, restoring you, correcting you, and comforting you. He will never give up on you, no matter how often you fail. He will keep teaching you, guiding you, restoring you, correcting you, and comforting you. So the next time you feel condemned, remember it is from the devil and then run to God. Ask him for help, because no matter how bad you messed up or failed, he is waiting for you with open arms.

Additional verses to meditate on:

"Then was Jesus led up of the Spirit into the wilderness to be tempted of the devil. And when he had fasted forty days and forty nights, he was afterward an hungred. And when the tempter came to him, he said, If thou be the Son of God, command that these stones be made bread. But he answered and said, It is written, Man shall not live by bread alone, but by every word that proceedeth out of the mouth of God." Matthew 4:1-4

"For God so loved the world, that he gave his only begotten Son, that whosoever believeth in him should not perish, but have everlasting life. For God sent not his Son into the world to condemn the world; but that the world through him might be saved." John 3:16-17

"Wherefore take unto you the whole armour of God, that ye may be able to withstand in the evil day, and having done all, to stand. Stand therefore, having your loins girt about with truth, and having on the breastplate of righteousness; And your feet shod with the preparation of the gospel of peace; Above all, taking the shield of faith, wherewith ye shall be able to quench all the fiery darts of the wicked." Ephesians 6:13-16

"Submit yourselves therefore to God. Resist the devil, and he will flee from you." James 4:7

"Be sober, be vigilant; because your adversary the devil, as a roaring lion, walketh about, seeking whom he may devour." 1 Peter 5:8

Chapter 24

LET GOD TAKE CARE OF YOU

"Humble yourselves therefore under the mighty hand of God, that he may exalt you in due time: Casting all your care upon him; for he careth for you."
1 Peter 5:6-7

There will come a time in your walk with God where you will say something like this to him, "God, I'm tired and wore out. I'm done trying to do it all. I'm done trying to figure it all out. I'm done trying to change myself. God, I give it all to you. It's now all in your hands." Once you come to this place in your walk with God, you will find true peace, because you have finally stopped your own efforts of trying to change yourself, of trying to make things happen, of trying to figure it all out. This is when God steps in all the way and takes over. Now if you are like me, doing nothing to make yourself better will be extremely hard for you, because you feel you should be doing something. You feel that if you do not do something, nothing will happen. But God has taught me that I need to remain at rest and to let him take care of me. God has it all under control. If he wants you to do something, he will let you know. Learn to let God take care of you.

God wants to take care of you. He wants you to look only to him as your source of supply. God may use your paycheck from work as the channel to supply your needs, but your employer is just the channel for God's provision. God can shift to another channel any time he wants. When you start to look to something or someone else to meet your needs, you are looking at the channel and not the source. The danger in this is if the channel dries up, you will worry. For example, if you are looking to your job as the source instead of the channel and something happens at your workplace which may lead to you losing your job, you will worry. But if you are looking at your job as the channel God is using to provide for you and you lose your job, you will not worry because your source, God, is still active and providing for you. When God turns off one channel, he can turn on another one. Bring God all of your needs. Let him choose whatever channel he chooses to fulfill your need. It may be a channel different than you choose. In fact, God may deliberately choose a different channel in order to teach you to keep looking to him for all of your needs. God alone is the source of your supply.

God wants you to believe he will take care of you. Here is a testimony from my life. I have extremely bad allergies. Pollen season is a particularly hard time of year for me. One year as I was planning my annual trip to Texas to visit my mom, I was looking for an airline mileage ticket to fly out in July. I only had 25,000 miles in my Alaska Airlines mileage account and the only mileage ticket available in July was for 65,000 miles. The only other time I was able to take off of work was in May, so I checked and there was a mileage ticket in May for 25,000 miles, so May it was. Two days before I was to fly back home to Fairbanks, Alaska, I checked the pollen count. It was 4198! I thought to myself, "If it is that high when I get home, I will probably land out in the hospital or something." I had never seen the pollen count that high before. The normal was around 1500 and about eight years ago it got up to 3000, which was a real bad year for me. I prayed and asked God to either lower the pollen count or let me be able to handle it when I got back home. The next day I checked the pollen count again and it went down to 643. Praise the Lord! I was so excited. God not only answered my prayer, but a pollen count of 4198 going down to 643 is a miracle to me. After I got home, I pondered the whole trip and I realized God knew the pollen count would be that high on that day in May. In his infinite wisdom, he made sure I flew to Texas in May instead of July. God took care of me. God will take care of you.

God will always take care of you. If he wants you to have something, you will have it. Here is another testimony from my life. On the first floor of the building where I work, there was an office full of framed prints that our security guard, Ted was selling. Ted had been collecting these prints over several years and was now displaying them in his office. One day as I was walking past his office, my eye caught a glimpse of one of his prints. I just noticed the top portion of the picture, but it intrigued me. It was a man in a suit sitting in a leather lounge chair and he looked discouraged. He was holding his head in one of his hands. I really wanted to know why he was so discouraged. I thought to myself that I need to stop to get a better look, but did not have the time right then. This happened a few times, but then one day I was walking by his office again. This time the print was on an easel and for the first time I saw the whole picture. The bottom half of the print was Jesus washing this man's feet. I just stood there staring at the picture. Tears welled up in my eyes. I could not believe how much this picture moved me. I was standing there thinking about how much God loves me. Jesus (God in the flesh), our Creator, is washing this man's feet because he was discouraged. I know it was just a symbol, but to me it was a powerful message. The print was a painting by Ron DiCianni called, "The Servant." I really wanted to have that print. No picture has ever moved me like this one. In my mind, I saw the picture hanging over my desk in my office at home. But then I noticed the price tag, $750. My heart sank because I did not have peace about asking my husband for $750 for a print for my office. That evening I told my husband about the framed print. He said it would be much cheaper if we could find a print and get it framed ourselves. The next day I told Ted about how much this print moved me and he said if I really wanted it, he would sell it to me for $250. I could not believe my ears. That is what it would have probably cost to get a print framed. I called my husband right away and my husband said to go ahead and write a check. I ran down to Ted's office with a check in hand and a few minutes later I was walking up to my office with the framed print in hand. That evening my husband hung the print over my desk in my office at home. It looked beautiful. When I think back on all that happened, I knew God wanted me to have that framed print. God is always so good to us.

You do not even have to worry about how you are going to learn all God wants you to learn from the Bible. God will not only reveal things to you while you are reading his Word and talking to him, he will also direct you to books he wants you to read, programs he wants you to watch, songs he wants you to listen to and sermons he wants you to listen to, besides the ones you are already hearing at church. I am always amazed how everything I am reading, watching, and listening to ties in with what God is teaching me at the moment.

When God wanted me to learn about how much he loves me, he led me to a set of sermons on the book Songs of Solomon. I thought this book in the Bible was about the love between a husband and wife, but I had never heard anyone preach on this book. After I found these sermons on the Internet, I listened to a couple of them and felt in my heart God wanted me to listen to all of them. There were many sermons. They were each about one hour long, so I would often think about them, but did not have time to just stop and listen to them. Then one day God put on my heart to download these sermons to my iTunes and then snyc them to my iPod and listen to them on the airplane when I would be flying to San Francisco for work in a few weeks. In the meantime, my laptop broke and it took two weeks for it to get repaired. When I finally got it back, it was only a week away from my trip. I finally sat down to download the sermons. I was having a terrible time trying to figure out how to download the sermons, and I remember thinking to myself that if God wants me to listen to these sermons, it will happen. And right after that thought, I figured out how to download the sermons. The moment I stopped trying to figure out how to download the sermons and just trusted that God would step in at any time if this was his will for me, that is the moment God stepped in.

Spend time with God every day. Let God take care of you. Give him all of your cares. Thank him for his love, mercy, and patience. Trust him. Look for his goodness every day. Be led by his Spirit. God will take care of you.

Additional verses to meditate on:

"The steps of a good man are ordered by the LORD: and he delighteth in his way. Though he fall, he shall not be utterly cast down: for the LORD upholdeth him with his hand. I have been young and now am old; yet have I not seen the righteous forsaken, nor his seed begging bread." Psalm 37:23-25

"For as many of you as have been baptized into Christ have put on Christ. There is neither Jew nor Greek, there is neither bond nor free, there is neither male nor female: for ye are all one in Christ Jesus. And if ye be Christ's, then are ye Abraham's seed, and heirs according to the promise." Galatians 3:27-29

"But now thus saith the Lord that created thee, O Jacob, and he that formed thee, O Israel, Fear not: for I have redeemed thee, I have called thee by thy name; thou art mine. When thou passest through the waters, I will be with thee; and through the rivers, they shall not overflow thee: when thou walkest through the fire, thou shalt not be burned; neither shall the flame kindle upon thee. For I am the Lord thy God, the Holy One of Israel, thy Saviour: I gave Egypt for thy ransom, Ethiopia and Seba for thee." Isaiah 43:1-3

"If any of you lack wisdom, let him ask of God, that giveth to all men liberally, and upbraideth not; and it shall be given him. But let him ask in faith, nothing wavering. For he that wavereth is like a wave of the sea driven with the wind and tossed. For let not that man think that he shall receive any thing of the Lord." James 1:5-7

"Wherefore seeing we also are compassed about with so great a cloud of witnesses, let us lay aside every weight, and the sin which doth so easily beset us, and let us run with patience the race that is set before us." Hebrews 12:1

Chapter 25

A HELPFUL CHECKLIST

"O Lord our Lord, how excellent is thy name in all the earth! who hast set thy glory above the heavens." Psalm 8:1

If you do not like checklists, then feel free to skip this chapter. But if you like checklists like I do, then you will love this list. I created this checklist for myself to keep my day on track. I pray you will find it helpful.

1. <u>EARNESTLY SEEK GOD EVERY DAY THROUGH PRAYER</u>. Prayer is powerful. It opens the door for God and his angels to work. In Psalm 78:61, it says God has delivered his strength into captivity, so he cannot work until you pray. Tell God what is on your heart. Thank him for all his goodness.

2. <u>BRING ALL OF YOUR CARES TO JESUS</u>. Leave them with him and walk away with his rest.

3. <u>LET NOT YOUR HEART BE TROUBLED.</u> Do this one thing and the Lord will take care of everything else. He will take care of you, your ministry, your family. He will take care of everything that needs taken care of. Why, because if your heart is not troubled, you are trusting him. As long as you let not your heart be troubled, the grace of God flows but as soon as you are troubled, the grace in that area stops.

SO NO MATTER WHAT IS TROUBLING YOU, SAY, "IT IS WELL WITH MY SOUL."

4. EARNESTLY SEEK GOD EVERY DAY BY READING HIS WORD. Read God's Word every day because his words are more powerful than a twoedged sword and worth more than all the fine gold in the world. Reading God's Word will renew your mind by exchanging the lies this world has fed you with God's truth. As you read about Jesus and behold his grace and beauty, you will transform into his image effortlessly.

5. MEDITATE ON GOD'S WORD. Think about God's Word throughout the day. Sing Scripture songs out loud or in your mind. Ponder what you read. Ask God questions about his Word.

6. LISTEN FOR GOD'S VOICE IN YOUR SPIRIT - God will speak to you in many different ways. Do not just talk to him, listen for his voice. While you are reading his Word, listen with your spirit. Sometimes he will teach you something. Sometimes he will ask you to do something. Sometimes he will correct you. Sometimes he just stirs up your spirit about something. You will know it is God's voice, because his voice will lead you and guide you into all truth, but the devil's voice will drive you, force you, or manipulate you.

7. LISTEN TO AND SING SONGS ABOUT JESUS, because what you hear affects how you think. In Isaiah 26:3, it says to keep your mind stayed on God and he will keep you in perfect peace. One way to keep your mind on God is to sing or listen to songs about him.

8. DO NOT TRY TO CHANGE YOURSELF. Read God's Word, so your thoughts will be replaced by his thoughts. You will be transformed by renewing your mind with his Word (Romans 12:2). You will be transformed by beholding Jesus, because the Bible says as he is, so are we in this world (1 John 4:17). As you are spending time with him and in his Word,

his Spirit fills your spirit and when you respond, it will be him responding through you. As you are filling your mind with his words, God's thoughts are replacing your thoughts. Talk to God, read his Word, sing Scriptures songs and hymns, listen to songs about Jesus, and listen to Bible preaching, because while you are doing these things, God will tell you exactly what he wants to address in your life and it will not overwhelm you. It will most likely be one thing at a time. He is kind, patient, and merciful. He will work with you, teach you, guide you, and open your eyes to see things you have never seen before. Be patient with God and yourself because transformation takes time.

9. Tell yourself <u>GOD LOVES YOU UNCONDITIONALLY</u> until you believe it with all of your heart. Once you have grasped the truth of God's unconditional love, it will put an end to all the fear in your life, because you know he is with you and he is for you and that whatever happens in your life, he will make it work out for good.

10. If you believe in Jesus, <u>YOU HAVE RIGHT STANDING WITH GOD</u>. God's love for you is not based on what you do, it is based on what Jesus has done. You can come boldly to God's throne and tell him whatever is on your heart. If you messed up and feel like God does not love you anymore, ignore your feelings and believe what God's Word says. God loves you! He will never leave you! If you messed up and feel like running away from God, don't. Run to him and he will be there with open arms. Be very careful about how you think about yourself. The Bible says that through the blood of Christ we have been completely cleansed and that we stand righteous before God clothed not in our own righteousness, but his. As he is (Jesus), so are we in this world.

11. <u>WAIT ON THE LORD</u> and do not go ahead of him. Do not try to do it on your own without his leading. If you have prayed about something or God put something on your heart

and it is not coming to pass, keep waiting on God. Before you do anything, ask yourself, "Am I being motivated by God or by my flesh."

12. All good things come from God and all evil things come from the devil, but <u>GOD PROMISED TO WORK ALL THINGS OUT FOR GOOD</u> (Romans 8:28) and whatever evil he cannot work out for good, he will restrain (Psalm 76:10). If you really believe this, then nothing should annoy you, because you know whatever comes your way during your day is there for a reason. It came your way because God gave it permission to be there. Look for God's hand in everything and ask him what he wants you to learn.

13. <u>THE JOY OF THE LORD IS YOUR STRENGTH.</u> Get your strength from knowing you are the joy of the Lord, because if your strength is linked to your performance, you will live a life that is constantly interchanging from being a self-righteous Pharisee one minute when you think you are doing well to a miserable wretch the next when you think you have failed.

14. <u>GUARD YOUR HEART</u> because whatever is in your heart comes out of your life. *"Keep thy heart (your inner life) with all diligence; for out of it are the issues of life." Proverbs 4:23 "Blessed are the pure in heart, for they shall see God." Matthew 5:8.* Your real life is what is going on inside of you, not what is going on around you.

15. <u>DO NOT RESPOND TO CRITICISM.</u> Let the Lord defend you. The battle is the Lord's.

16. <u>NEVER GIVE UP.</u> Even though you are suffering, keep pressing on. Do not ever give up, because the end results are love, joy, peace, longsuffering, gentleness, goodness, faith, meekness, and temperance.

17. <u>WHEN YOU GET DISCOURAGED, ENCOURAGE YOURSELF IN THE LORD</u> by talking to him, singing to him, praising him, thanking him, and by reading his Word.

And remember, you are never going to be what God wants you to be if you do not stop being mad at yourself because you are not what you think you should be right now.

18. <u>THE HOLY SPIRIT IS LIVING INSIDE OF YOU</u> which means you have everything you need to do what God is asking you to do. He will never leave you or forsake you.

19. <u>HAVE CONFIDENCE IN CHRIST AND NOT YOURSELF</u>, because if you have confidence in yourself, you will do things without praying which means you are doing things in your own strength. But if you pray and ask God to help you, it will be God working through you and that will produce Godly fruit. Remember, at the judgment seat you will only get rewarded for things God has done through you. All the things you have done on your own (in the flesh, by your own strength) will be burned up as wood, hay, and stubble (1 Corinthians 3:12–15).

20. <u>TELL YOUR NEEDS TO JESUS AND LET HIM ALONE MEET THEM.</u> Do not try to get your needs met by others. Be dependent on God and not on people or on yourself. Ask and you will receive, but you have to believe and wait on God, trusting it will come in his time. The more we need God, the more we experience his nearness and his power in our lives.

21. <u>BEWARE OF YOUR THOUGHTS</u>. You can choose what you think about. Think on these things: whatsoever things are true, honest, just, pure, lovely, and of a good report (Philippians 4:8). If you stay busy thinking about right things, the devil will not be able to fill your mind with wrong things.

22. <u>IF YOU ARE STRUGGLING OR FEELING FRUSTRATED, IT MEANS YOU ARE TRYING TO DO SOMETHING IN THE FLESH.</u> Give your struggles to God immediately. And if the devil whispers in your ear, "What are you going to do about it? What are you going to

do about it? What are you going to do about it?" Tell him, "Nothing at all." You need to stop trying to do something about something you cannot do anything about. You need to stop trying to get rid of things only God can get rid of. And you need to stop trying to get all these things that you are never going to get unless God decides to give them to you.

23. <u>REMAIN STABLE</u>, because that means you are trusting God. This is one of the best things you can do to defeat the devil, remain calm no matter what is going on around you. Refuse to let your soul get up and start running around. Refuse to get emotionally distraught. Refuse to get into worrying and reasoning.

24. <u>GOD HAS A PLAN FOR YOU</u> but you have to spend time with God and in his Word in order for you to see that plan come to pass. So read his Word, study it, sing it, and meditate on it.

25. <u>THE POWER OF LIFE AND DEATH ARE IN THE TONGUE</u>. Watch what comes out of your mouth. Every time you open your mouth, you either increase or decrease your power. Your words have power in the spirit realm.

26. <u>YOU HAVE BEEN ASSIGNED ANGELS TO PROTECT YOU</u>, but angels only hearken unto God and his Word. They are only moved by God and his Word. They are only motivated by God and his Word. So stop murmuring and complaining. Stop grumbling and gossiping. Stop finding fault and tale bearing. Start praising God. Start thanking God. Say God's Word out loud. This gives your angels something to work with. Words have power in the spirit realm.

27. <u>THE DEVIL WANTS TO KILL YOUR BODY, STEAL YOUR PEACE, AND DESTROY YOUR LIFE</u>. The devil wants your peace, because if he can upset you and get your mind off of God, he has won. He does this by attacking your mind. That is why God says in his Word to take every thought captive, so if you have wrong thoughts, thoughts

that do not line up with God's Word, do not entertain them. Think good thoughts on purpose. As you read and study God's Word, your mind will be filled with God's thoughts and this will help you to immediately recognize thoughts that come into your mind that are not truth.

28. <u>IT IS ALL ABOUT JESUS</u>. Remember, you are who and what you are only by God's grace. It is his power and strength added to your weakness. It is his righteousness that you have, not your own. So when your flesh rises up and thinks it is something, ignore it. Remember your righteousness is as filthy rags. It is all about Jesus. You have one job to do and that is to glorify God. He gets all the glory.

29. <u>KEEP YOUR FOCUS ON JESUS</u>, because whatever you focus on grows. If you focus on the positive, the positive gets bigger. If you focus on the negative, the negative gets bigger. If you focus on your disease, lack, troubles, addictions and weaknesses, they will only get bigger. Focus only on Jesus, the author and finisher of your faith.

30. <u>BE LED BY GOD'S SPIRIT</u>. Listen for his voice in your heart. Be led by God's peace. If you do not have peace in your heart about doing something, then don't do it.

31. <u>THIS IS THE BEST DAY OF YOUR LIFE</u>, because God designed it just for you. This is the day the Lord hath made. Rejoice and be glad in it.

Chapter 26

A DAY IN MY LIFE WITH GOD

"O the depth of the riches both of the wisdom and knowledge of God! how unsearchable are his judgments, and his ways past finding out! For who hath known the mind of the Lord? or who hath been his counsellor? Or who hath first given to him, and it shall be recompensed unto him again? For of him, and through him, and to him, are all things: to whom be glory for ever. Amen." Romans 11:33-36

I decided to make the last chapter A DAY IN MY LIFE WITH GOD. In the summer of 2010, I kept a daily journal/blog of my walk with God. I am thinking about publishing these journal/blog entries in a book one day. I love to hear about other people's walk with God. It is encouraging to me. It gives me ideas about my own walk. In this chapter, I chose three entries from my journal/blog. I decided to include these journal entries as a chapter to give you an idea of how I interact with God throughout my day. Since these journal/blog entries are from about four years ago, I am amazed as I read over them now how much God has taught me since then. You might not have time to write down as much detail about your walk with God every day, but I want to encourage you to write down what you can. You will be amazed after you go back and read what you wrote of what God has done in your life. Our God is an amazing God!

Friday, July 30, 2010

Me reading the Bible: Psalm 149-150, Proverbs 30, Leviticus 19, Scripture song Isaiah 26:3

Proverbs 30:5, "Every word of God is pure; he is a shield unto them that put their trust in him." I love that - every word of God is pure! Other verses say your word is better than silver and fine gold, more powerful than a twoedged sword, profitable for doctrine, reproof, correction, and for instruction in righteousness. Father, you know I buy a lot of books, because I love to read. I've always told myself that if I get just one good piece of advice, or a good recipe, anything like that, from one of the books that I've bought, then it was worth the price I paid for it. Putting all this into perspective, Father, if every word in the Bible is profitable, your Word is worth more than all the gold in the world. If I really believed this, I would read it more. In fact, I do need to read it more, especially more than other books. Thank you, Father, for helping me put all this into perspective.

The word "shield" reminds me of the Star Trek Enterprise. When its shield was up, the enemy's shots or even the universe's rocks couldn't get through to the Enterprise. So you are saying, Father, that if I trust in you, you will be a shield around me so my enemies or even the world can't hurt me? That's awesome! Father, I need to learn to trust you more. Help me. Teach me. Actually, I was watching Joyce Meyer's program last night and she said something that might help me in this area. She said it took her a whole year of studying your Word and pretty much every morning standing in front of the mirror saying to herself, "God loves me." She said she did this until one day she got it. She felt it. She knew it without a doubt. I think that is what I need to do until I learn to trust you fully. I need to tell myself every day that I trust you for all my needs and I also need to study all that your Word has to say about trust. That's what I'm going to do, Father. I'm going to write in a notebook every verse that has to do with trusting you until I get it. Until I know without a doubt that you will take care of me and I don't have to worry about a thing. I need to let my guard down, so your shield can go up.

Leviticus 19:31, "Regard not them that have familiar spirits, neither seek after wizards, to be defiled by them: I am the LORD your God." I seem to remember from Tom Sooter's sermons that familiar spirits are evil spirits familiar with a person's ancestral past, but I just read a little more about this on the Spiritual Warfare and Deliverance Ministry site and it said that familiar spirits applies to the practice of communicating with the spirits of the dead. It also said, "the practice involved sorcerers, mediums, or necromancers, who professed to call up the dead to answer questions. These individuals were said to have a 'familiar spirit' of another dead person. In fact, the different voice that came out of a person claiming to call the dead was not that of a dead person but that of a demon spirit. Any apparition was also the work of demons. A demon spirit can fake the voice or image of a dead person." Father, this latter explanation actually reminds me of something I read in a book called, "The Bondage Breaker." The pastor who wrote this book discovered, while he was talking to a demon through the person the demon was possessing, that demons cannot say things like "Jesus is their Lord," but they can say it if the "dead" person they are impersonating was a Christian. Father, I guess it doesn't matter if familiar spirits are generational spirits or spirits familiar with the lives of dead people. The bottom line is that they are evil spirits and we need to stay away from them.

Me after lunch: Father, as I was flossing my teeth after lunch, I was thinking again on how I can't wait to get all these food particles out of my teeth because they really bother me and then my mind thought about the other day when you told me about how the Bible is kind of like floss. You have all these food particles (stuff that shouldn't be there) in your life, but you don't feel them until you start reading the Bible. After we start reading your Word, we start feeling the food particles in our lives that should not be there and then we can't wait to get them out. As I was thinking this, Father, I felt you put on my heart:

God: But there's a difference between food particles in your teeth and food particles in your life. The food particles in your teeth can be taken out quickly with floss, but the food particles in your life will take a lot longer. You need to be patient with me, other people, and yourself, because I am working with people's hearts and that takes time. I am working in people's lives and that takes time. It takes time to undo wrong thinking, wrong teachings, hurts, failures, and frustrations people have in their heart. It takes time for people to let go and trust me.

Me: Thank you, Father, for being patient with us.

Me: Father, it's been another wonderful day and I'm looking forward to a busy, but fun weekend.

Sunday, August 1, 2010

Me: Father, thank you so much for preachers who are on fire for you. This morning during the church service, for the first time ever, I just wanted to get up and shout. I was so excited inside. I wanted to say, where do I sign up. God, I feel a stirring in my heart that I've never felt before. I know my book and blog ministry is geared toward Christians, but I want to be a part of the harvest. I want to lead people to Christ every day. Father, open doors for me, because right now all I see are closed doors.

God: They will be opened when the time is right. I'm just stirring up your heart, so you will be ready to run when I open the doors.

Me: I will wait on you, Father, because my hope is only in you. I can't get over of what is happening inside of me. I can't get over the changes in my heart and in my life. I haven't done a thing except seek your face every day and obey what you are putting on my heart to do. Well, maybe not obeying everything you are putting on my heart to do, but you are working on that. My flesh still steps in way too often, but I know you are working on that also. You really are putting desires in my heart, so that I actually want to do what you are putting on my heart to do. It's just amazing. I am so glad you put on my heart to write it all down every day, because I never want to forget what you are doing and how you did it. My prayer, Father, is for my children and grandchildren, and anyone who reads what you are doing in my life, my prayer is that they will catch this fire you have put in my heart. My prayer is that they will want to seek you everyday, to get to know you and what you have planned just for them. My prayer is that they will start a daily walk with you. And one more very important thing, Father, which took a little while for me to understand, my prayer is that you will put in everyone's heart who starts walking toward you, that they will not have to change a thing about themselves. All they have to do is start walking towards you by talking to you everyday and reading your Word, because you are the Word, and you will take over from here. You will show them what they need to do or not do. You will change them and start working through them. Father, it will all be you and you will get all the glory. Thank you so much, Father, for teaching me this. Today during church, I heard myself saying that I want to be like that. I want to make that change in my life, but then you quickly reminded me that I cannot change me. So Father, I am asking you to please change me. Mold me into what you want me to be. Work through me so your will for my life will be accomplished daily through me.

Me: Father, the preacher today said something that I don't ever want to forget, so I'll close my entry today with his words, "This is going to be the best day of your life, because it was designed by God just for you. This is the day the Lord hath made. Rejoice and be glad in it."

Wednesday, August 18, 2010

Me reading the Bible: I read Song of Solomon 6-8, Psalm 1-3, Proverbs 18, and 1 John 1-2, and I sang Psalm 1.

Here is what caught my attention while reading your Word today:

In Proverbs 18:21, it says, *"Death and life are in the power of the tongue: and they that love it shall eat the fruit thereof."* Kind of like eating your words? Father, I was listening to Joyce Meyer's program last night and she was talking about the power of the tongue and how powerful our words are, especially those words we say between prayers. It never ceases to amaze me that when you are teaching me something, everything I read and programs I watch all seem to be leading me down the same path, everything just seems to tie together. Father, when Joyce said something to the effect that we use our tongue to praise God and curse men. Actually, she said that's in the Bible. I think in James. Right after she said that, I said to myself, "No, I don't." And you said in my heart:

God: Yes, you do. Every time a car on the road does something to upset you, like pull in front of you, you curse them.

Me: You are right. You are always right. I need to watch not only my thoughts, but the words that come out of my mouth.

"Love not the world, neither the things that are in the world. If any man love the world, the love of the Father is not in him. For all that is in the world, the lust of the flesh, and the lust of the eyes, and the pride of life, is not of the Father, but is of the world. And the world passeth away, and the lust thereof: but he that doeth the will of God abideth for ever." 1 John 2:15-17.

Father, I know this is what you are working on in my life. You are teaching me to live a more frugal life and not to lust after things I don't need. You are teaching me that you hate pride and don't want it in my life at all. You are teaching me to control my appetites and to eat simple meals.

"And now, little children, abide in him; that, when he shall appear, we may have confidence, and not be ashamed before him at his coming." 1 John 28. Father, teach me how to abide in you.

God: Read more of my words. Spend more time with me.

Me during lunch: Father, I was thinking about this Clint Eastwood movie where he was a sergeant that was put in charge of a unit and when he got through working with them, they were very disciplined young men, and as I was thinking about this, I felt you put on my heart:

God: Boot camp can be likened to what I do with the lives of those who let me work in them. I don't force anyone to do anything, but if they let me, I work in their lives so that one day they will say, "Yes, Sir," to anything I tell them to do.

Me: Father, thank you for answering my call of help to understand the book of Song of Solomon. Why am I always surprised when you answer my prayers? Last week I was on Zachary's facebook page and I found a sermon by Leonard Ravenhill entitled, "Agony." It so stirred up my soul that I wanted to find more sermons like that one. Your Word does say we need to stir ourselves up in you, and I find one way for doing this is listening to powerful sermons. So yesterday I googled Leonard Ravenhill and it took me to http://www.puritanfellowship.com/ because they had a page with lots of Leonard Ravenhill's quotes. Today I went back to that page because I saw many interesting titles that caught my attention and when I scrolled down the page, there it was. Your answer to my prayer. It was a whole list of sermons on Song of Solomon. I already listened to two of them and they were powerful. I learned that Song of Solomon is about "a series of breathtaking parables and allegories about the passionate love between the God man, Jesus Christ and his bride, the believers, the church." I actually took some notes of one of the sermons because it so stirred up a desire in me to get to know God better, to get all my joy from him and nothing else. Here is where this sermon is: http://www.puritanfellowship.com/2010/05/song-of-solomon-sermon-series-kevin.html and here are some powerful notes I took:

Your growth as a Christian is totally dependent upon Christ. You must get this because when you are confident in your own strength, you will do things prayerlessly. When you have confidence in the flesh, you will do things in the flesh. But the more you realize that you are totally dependent upon God to do any good in this life, the more you will be on your knees before God in prayer.

The Lord will direct you <u>when</u> you don't lean on your own understanding. Proverbs 3

What we do reveals what we really believe. Faith without works is dead.

The single object of your joy should be Christ. If your joy is linked to your performance, then you will just live a life constantly interchanging from being a self-righteous Pharisee one minute when you think you are doing well or a miserable wretch the next, when you think you are failing.

It is only by us bringing to remembrance the love of Christ, of what he has done for us that we will walk in a clear conscience before him. It is only by remembering Christ's great love for us that we will be careful not to carry on in sin. We love him because he first loved us. It is by remembering his love towards us that we become upright, that we become more like him. It's not the other way around. We don't make ourselves more upright, so we deserve more of his love. If you turn your Christianity into nothing more than a long list of rules and regulations, then that will rob you of your joy. You will be miserable because all that type of behavior will do anyway is stir up more sin in you and you constantly have a Pharisee equal attitude towards others who are not living up to your standard, even though in reality, you are not really living up to it yourself. It does not say here that you will remember your love for Christ more than wine as some self-righteous Pharisee priding himself and being judgmental towards other people. It says we will remember his love.

Me: All I can say is Wow! Thank you so much for steering me towards that site today, Father. I plan on visiting this site daily until you tell me to stop.

Made in the USA
Middletown, DE
18 January 2025